Microcomputer Management & Maintenance for Libraries

Supplements to
COMPUTERS IN LIBRARIES

Microcomputer Management & Maintenance for Libraries

Elizabeth S. Lane

Meckler

Westport • London

Library of Congress Cataloging-in-Publication Data

Lane, Elizabeth S.
    Microcomputer management & maintenance for libraries / by
Elizabeth S. Lane
        p. cm. -- (Supplements to computers in libraries ; 16)
    Includes bibliographical references and index.
    ISBN 0-88736-522-1 (alk. paper) : $
    1. Microcomputers -- Library applications. 2. Microcomputers -
- Maintenance and repair. 3. Libraries -- Automation -- Management.
I. Title. II. Title: Microcomputer management and maintenance for
libraries. III. Series.
Z678.93.M53L36   1990
025'.00285'416--dc20   90-6342
                                              CIP

British Library Cataloguing in Publication Data

Lane, Elizabeth S.
    Microcomputer management & maintenance for libraries.
    1. Libraries. Microcomputer systems. Management
    I. Title
    025.00285416

    ISBN 0-88736-522-1

Meckler Corporation, 11 Ferry Lane West, Westport, CT 06880.
Meckler Ltd., Grosvenor Gardens House, Grosvenor Gardens,
    London SW1W 0BS, U.K.

Printed on acid free paper.
Printed and bound in the United States of America.

Contents

Appendices

Preface

This book grew out of a panel presentation given at the Meckler 1988 *Small Computers in Libraries* conference in Chicago, where Sally Small of the University of Pennsylvania had asked me to speak on preventive maintenance for microcomputers. Our suspicion that the issue of microcomputer maintenance was more important to library managers than the volume of current literature suggested turned out to be correct; the level of interest that our panel presentation generated demonstrated a strong unmet need for more information on this topic as it related to the library and information science world.

Soon after the conference, Anthony Abbott of Meckler Corporation contacted me to propose a book on microcomputer maintenance. As we discussed the project, it became clear that the issue of maintenance needed to be addressed within the broader context of computer management issues. Maintenance and management are so closely linked that a book addressing one and not the other would be less likely to meet the needs of many library managers currently facing the tasks of evaluating, purchasing, installing, and maintaining microcomputer facilities for their staff and their patrons. Although no one book can begin to address all the challenges that individual managers will face as they move into the age of automation, I have attempted to give a comprehensive overview of the information necessary to effectively manage a library microcomputer facility.

Much of the information I share with you in this book has come to me through the wonders of electronic communication. I would like to give much-deserved credit for many of the ideas presented here to the members of ALIX, the computer bulletin board for Federal librarians run from the office of FedLink at the Library of Congress; to the members of the Twilight Clone, the primary Macintosh technical bulletin board in the Washington, D.C. area; and to the participants of several *Confer II*™ computer conferences on the University of Michigan MTS computer system. These people shared with me much of the wealth of their experience and accumulated knowledge; in many cases, all I have done is distilled their wisdom for you. (Phone numbers and enrollment information for these services are listed in Appendix D; the usefulness of participation in these electronic forums is discussed at greater length in Chapter 1.)

Thanks go also to two of my former colleagues at the Library of Congress, John Ragsdale and Felix Krayeski of the CRS Automation Office, and two of my current colleagues at Congressional Information Service, Bob Starbird and Andy Ross. Without the benefit of their extensive technical knowledge, and their faith in my abilities, I would not have found the confidence I needed to start or complete this book.

My stepfather, Don Reinfeld, put forth an extraordinary effort in editing drafts of the book on short notice; the incorporation of his many suggestions has made this a far better text.

Anthony Abbott of Meckler Corporation is responsible for taking this book from an idle speculation in my mind to an actual publication by his company. I am grateful to him for his belief in my skills and knowledge, for his patience with my delays, and for his support of my efforts.

Finally, without my husband, Davison Tudder, this book would never have been completed. His encouragement of my efforts and confidence in my capabilities are the reasons this book made it into print.

Thank you all.

Introduction

Since their introduction in the early 1980s, personal computers—or microcomputers—have quickly become vital components of libraries and information centers. Their proliferation has greatly enhanced productivity in library environments, and has enabled library users to access more information in more formats than ever before. At the same time, however, it has resulted in a host of new issues to be dealt with at every level of library management.

What sets the use of microcomputers in libraries or information centers apart from their use in business environments is the dual purpose the microcomputer can play in libraries. In most businesses, microcomputers are used primarily to automate the basic administrative tasks that are performed to keep the office running smoothly—bookkeeping, word processing, database management. In library settings, however, microcomputers are used not only as administrative or clerical workstations, but also as "information stations," enabling both library staff and library patrons to access a growing world of electronically stored information.

This duality of purpose adds a number of factors to each level of decision making in microcomputer management. Managers need to take into account the needs of both staff and patrons, as well as considering a wider range of hardware and software options. Compatibility and networking can be key issues, as it may or may not be necessary for administrative and public access micros to be able to share programs and data. Funding may become more complex, as different accounts may need to be accessed for different microcomputer applications. For these reasons, among others, many otherwise comprehensive books on the topic of microcomputer management and maintenance in business or academic settings fail to address the broader range of concerns that library and information professionals must confront in this area.

This is one of a number of publications on the topic of microcomputers in libraries. What sets this book apart from many others on this topic is its design as a general purpose resource. It is a resource for those who need to address a broad range of microcomputer-related topics, and who require a guide which can serve as both an instructional tool— explaining the basic concepts in a readable manner, and as a reference source—allowing for quick and efficient retrieval of specific information on an ad-hoc basis. Many of the resources already available focus on narrower views of microcomputer technology: some cover the use of microcomputers for accomplishing specific tasks—cataloging, acquisitions, financial recordkeeping; some examine the use of microcomputer technology in very specific locations, often consisting primarily of compilations of case studies from various institutions; still others deal with the applications of a certain type or brand of microcomputer technology. In contrast, this book has been designed to equip you, the information professional, with all the tools necessary to effectively manage microcomputers in a library or information center environment. It lays out the specific issues and decisions involved in implementing any type of microcomputer technology, from the initial planning decisions to the ongoing maintenance of the machines.

Those who are new to administrative or management roles, particularly in the implementation of new technology of any kind, are encouraged to read the first section of the book, "Managing Microcomputer Facilities in Libraries," completely before beginning the initial decision making processes of needs assessment and cost analysis. The overall perspective gained from examining all the issues covered will be of assistance in the initial planning stages that precede purchase and installation.

Those who are unfamiliar with microcomputer technology are similarly encouraged to read thoroughly the second section of the book,

"Maintaining Microcomputer Facilities in Libraries," before setting up any schedule of preventive maintenance, and before signing maintenance contracts with outside providers. It is important to be familiar with the full range of microcomputer hardware and software components, and their fallibility, before committing scarce resources to maintenance and repair contracts.

Finally, those who have experience with both management and maintenance of micros in libraries may find this book most useful as a reference source, rather than as an instructive text. Both sections of the book include worksheets that can be photocopied and used in various stages of the planning process when upgrades, replacements, and reinforcements for current computers are being considered. The maintenance section, in particular, has been designed to be used as a trouble-shooting guide. The checklists for preventive and responsive maintenance should be helpful in setting up a regular program of cost-saving maintenance tasks, and in helping to identify specific hardware and software problems when they occur.

The rapid pace of change in microcomputer technology makes it impractical to write extensively about specific technologies or manufacturers. The few portions of this book that deal with the details of currently available hardware and software are sure to be obsolete soon after publication (if not even before publication). Therefore, the primary focus of the book is on the general topics that must be addressed regardless of the type of equipment being used. Some discussion of current technology is necessary to preserve the usefulness of the book as a practical management tool; however, the basic management issues have remained constant throughout the many changes in equipment specifications over the past decade, and are likely to endure for quite some time to come.

This book is not intended to serve as an introduction to the basic concepts of microcomputer technology. Those who have little or no background in the technical aspects of microcomputer use are encouraged to consult the bibliography in Appendix B of this book. A short glossary of technical terms used in this book does appear in Appendix A; however, this glossary should not be used in lieu of a basic textual introduction to this area of technology.

You will undoubtedly find yourself wanting to explore some of the topics presented in the book in more depth; for that reason, additional bibliographies of materials are contained in Appendix B. In addition, resources such as Microcomputer Index, Magazine Index, Library Literature, and Library and Information Science Abstracts will be useful tools in finding current literature on microcomputers in libraries. A list of journals focusing on microcomputer use in library environments is included in Appendix C. The changing nature of microcomputer technology tends to favor journal literature over monographic works for the effective communication of new information on equipment and applications. As a manager of a microcomputer facility, you will need to examine these journals, and make the decision of which to follow regularly. Suggestions for evaluation and selection of specific journals are also included in Appendix C.

As you become more familiar with microcomputer technology, joining a local microcomputer user group can be an excellent way to develop valuable contacts, and to receive advice and assistance from experienced microcomputer managers and users. These users groups can be formed around a specific technology (e.g., Macintosh or MS-DOS computers), or around a specific area of application (e.g., library or corporate users). Some information on locating and joining users groups is provided in Appendix D.

Chapter 1

Introduction to Managing Microcomputer Facilities in Libraries

Effective management of a microcomputer facility in a library or information center requires more than just a familiarity with current computer technology; it also requires a broad understanding of the multiple roles the library plays in its community, and of the many tasks that library staff must perform in support of these roles. Only a manager capable of integrating these disparate areas of knowledge will be able to design and run a successful facility. This portion of *Microcomputer Management & Maintenance for Libraries* is not meant to serve as a primary source of information for these topics. Instead, it is designed to provide you with a conceptual framework for managing a microcomputer facility. The information provided here will serve as the structure for your own management analysis. Within the general framework of this structure, you will need to supply the more specific information regarding equipment specifications and costs.

The key to effective microcomputer planning and management is effective information gathering. There are many resources available to those seeking to add to their knowledge and understanding of microcomputer technology and its potential role in the library or information center. Among the best sources of information can be other libraries in your area. Visits to other libraries can be one of the most valuable information-gathering tasks in the planning process. Through these visits, managers can determine what needs these other institutions have addressed through their use of microcomputer technology, examine the advantages and disadvantages of the environment in which they have housed their equipment, gain insight into the management problems they have faced during their planning for and implementation of the computers, and gather information on local vendors and the types of equipment available. The advice of other library administrators who have had to face the challenges of purchasing, installing, and managing microcomputer facilities is an invaluable resource, and should be sought actively; not just during the planning process, but whenever new questions about the management of microcomputer facilities arise.

Another valuable source of information can be local library associations, or the American Library Association. Two divisions of ALA that can be particularly helpful in assisting with management issues relating to automation in libraries are LITA (Library and Information Technology Association), and LAMA (Library Administration and Management Association). A list including the addresses of these groups, as well as other major U.S. and state library associations, appears in Appendix D.

Although libraries face a number of unique challenges in the area of automation, managers can nonetheless gain useful information from computer users from a variety of application areas. In many metropolitan areas, computer users have formed organizations, often called "users groups," to discuss specific types of microcomputer technology and applications. These groups may be focused on the use of a particular type of computer (for example, Apple II or IBM-PC users groups) or on the use of specific software applications (such as database users groups or even library microcomputer users groups).

Many users groups provide a service to their members called a bulletin board system. This is an electronic forum that can be accessed by using a computer and a modem. Participants can leave messages to each other, or to the group as a whole. Bulletin boards are also good sources of inexpensive public domain and "shareware" software. In addition to those bulletin board systems associated with users groups, a number of bulletin boards and similar sources of online information—some commercial, and some free of charge—are available to those interested in obtaining information on microcomputers via telecommunications.

Some of the better-known online information services are also listed in Appendix D. Participants in these national groups can often refer you to users groups and smaller bulletin board systems that are based in your geographic area. Keep in mind, however, that these groups can be quite ephemeral. Bulletin boards, in particular, often change phone numbers without warning.

Any investment in computer equipment, whether for a single microcomputer and printer for administrative use, or for a roomful of workstations networked together in a public access area, must begin with the careful consideration of a number of planning issues. When it begins with a carefully worked out plan, one which incorporates the input of staff and patrons, the automation process is far more likely to result in a successful, well-received microcomputer facility.

Once information has been gathered, and those staff members involved in the decision making have had the opportunity to learn the basics of computer technology as it relates to the library environment, the planning process moves on to the assessment of the library's actual needs: the needs of its managers, the needs of its staff, and most of all, the needs of its patrons. Work flow must be analyzed, weak points must be identified, and these needs must be mapped to the information gathered on current technology. Work space must also be examined, and the adaptability of the physical environment to the needs of electronic equipment must be assessed.

Planning activities then continue with the evaluation of all available resources. Sources for funding need to be identified and pursued; a working budget should be prepared which will allow the planners to identify practical solutions within the reach of the library's finances.

With this information on needs and funding, managers can then move on to identification of specific computer systems and software programs that meet the library's requirements for functionality and cost. The ever-expanding range of available computer systems make this step in the planning process one of the most difficult. Libraries must look not only at the ability of systems to meet their current needs, but also at the expandability and probable lifespan of the systems under inspection.

The process does not end with selection of specific hardware and software products. Managers must also prepare suitable environments for the new equipment, and institute appropriate procedures to safeguard the equipment and keep track of the software in use. In addition, there is the psychological preparation of staff members and library patrons for the many changes which automation can bring to library operations.

Because the planning process is so critical to the successful management of microcomputers in libraries, much of this management portion of the book is devoted to planning. Intertwined with these planning issues, of course, are the more practical management issues. Managing a microcomputer facility in a library can be a daunting task; a library administrator will find that along with the many advantages of automation come a host of challenges.

In order to ensure that a microcomputer facility continues runs smoothly after its installation, a manager must ensure that staff and patrons have been provided with adequate information on and preparation for the changes that will take place in the library environment. S/he must also institute a number of new routines, and involve all staff in the responsibility for the new activities related to automation. From the cataloging of software programs to the training of inquisitive patrons, library staff will need to take on a new variety of tasks and activities.

All of these planning and management topics are covered in this portion of the book: "Managing Microcomputer Facilities in Libraries." The topics have been arranged in the order in which they are normally encountered in the process of library automation, beginning with the basic steps of planning, and continuing through the processes of implementation and effective management. With the information provided here, a structure can be developed that should allow for the most effective and efficient purchase, installation, and use of the machines.

It is important to keep in mind, however, that one facet of managing microcomputers in libraries is maintaining those same computers. Although topics relating to microcomputer maintenance have been placed in the second section of this book, "Maintaining Microcomputer Facilities in Libraries," the issues brought up in those chapters should be considered by any manager planning for the implementation of microcomputer technology.

Chapter 2

The Planning Process

Planning has always been an integral part of a manager's responsibilities. When managing the selection and installation of microcomputers, however, it becomes crucial. Without a clear idea of their library's needs and resources, library administrators will be unable to select appropriate equipment. A lack of knowledge of available technology and its potential uses will also make it difficult for the manager to make effective choices that will enhance the library's ability to provide services. Only by carefully assessing needs and constraints, analyzing the costs and benefits of the prospective investment, and evaluating the range of available technology and equipment, can a library manager hope to take full advantage of the benefits of automation.

Many libraries, when considering the decisions involved with automation, choose to employ a consultant to provide advice on which computers to acquire and how to use them once they arrive. For libraries able to afford this type of assistance, whether it comes from an outside firm or an internal automation office, much of the information in this portion of the book will be superfluous—it will be the responsibility of the consultant to address the planning issues outlined here and in the chapters on needs assessment and cost analysis. However, it is in the best interest of the library manager to fully understand those issues, so s/he can provide the consultant with appropriate input and avoid the possibility of being saddled with a 'one size fits all' automation solution that may not be suited to the particular library environment at hand. Further, once the consultant has submitted his or her bill and moved on to another project, the library manager will still need to address the ongoing management issues that accompany the implementation and ongoing maintenance of automated solutions. The field of technology does not stand still, and today's automation investments will often need to be upgraded or replaced in the not-too-distant future.

This chapter discusses the preliminary steps of the planning process. Some of the topics discussed include the designation of automation planning team members, suggestions for potential sources of information to be used throughout your planning efforts, and a suggested timetable for a planning process.

The planning team

Although the final decision for any major purchase or change in workplace routines rests with the library director or manager, it is important for staff members to be involved in the decision-making process to as great an extent as possible. By involving staff, managers gain the insight of those who will actually be using the equipment. Since the decision to automate generally is based at least in part upon the desire to improve staff productivity, the opinions of those performing the tasks will be necessary in order to analyze the current workflow and identify areas where changes could have a positive effect upon staff productivity.

In addition to providing the manager with valuable information, staff members involved in the planning process are more likely to feel vested in the process of automation. With this sense of inclusion, employees are more likely to "buy into" the idea of automation, and to feel some degree of responsibility for the eventual success or failure of the automation effort. The importance of this sense of personal commitment is discussed at greater length in Chapter 7.

One of the most effective methods for involving staff at the start of your process is by forming a planning team, including at least one member of each department that will be affected by the use of the microcomputers. This guarantees input from a full range of areas within the library, and provides each area with an opportunity to voice their concerns throughout the planning process.

One possibility for the composition of the planning team is to include a manager from each area involved, as well as a non-supervisory employee who can give an operator-level perspective and provide a lateral link to employees who might otherwise feel shut out of the planning activities. It is easy for managers to forget that the greatest impact of the changes they are making will be felt by their staff; the inclusion of non-supervisory employees in the planning process will alleviate this problem. In addition, by providing for a mix of employees on the planning team, the manager makes it clear to staff members that all their opinions and ideas are highly valued in the management decision-making process.

The planning team can be involved in any or all of the management planning issues related to automating the library environment, from initial information gathering and needs assessment to determining staff needs and responsibilities. The team can have responsibility for information gathering, evaluation of options, and general advisory roles. The manager must determine the appropriate tasks for the team to participate in before the team has actually been formed. This decision should be based primarily upon the needs identified in the planning and implementation process. Will the team provide assistance in collecting information? In obtaining information about employee work patterns and needs? Or will it simply ensure that staff members are kept aware of the automation process as it proceeds? It is important to clearly define the role of the team when it is first formed, so as to avoid creating conflicts later on between group members' expectations and managerial constraints.

A regular schedule for team meetings should be developed, as advance notice of meeting dates enables members of the group to avoid problems in scheduling as the planning and installation proceeds. In addition, the specific responsibilities of individual group members— ranging from readings of selected literature to participation in library visits—should be codified and distributed, so that members can allocate sufficient time in their schedules to complete their tasks.

Information sources

In this first phase of planning, information gathering should be the highest priority. If the library is part of a larger institution or network, one of the first tasks should be to gather information from within that organization. Any existing systems or automation office, or computer center, should be contacted first. They can provide information about existing institutional guidelines for purchase and installation. Many public and academic library systems have already made an initial investment in a particular brand of computer equipment; it may then be necessary to conform to this institutional standard. If this is the case, access to institutional or group volume discounts from specific vendors may be available. Special librarians should consult with any MIS or computer support groups within their organization, or with their immediate supervisor, to determine if computer standards have already been set. If no branch or office has been charged with overseeing automation purchases, the library director (or an administrator at an equivalent level) should be consulted to determine whether other resources exist for support within the organization.

This is also the time to ensure that all participants in the planning process have a basic grounding in the areas of microcomputer technology and its potential application in library environments. Those completely unfamiliar with computers may want to start with a fairly general text; Peter McWilliams' books on computers and word processing are slightly out-of-date, but still provide a very clear and readable basic introduction to the basic concepts of microcomputers and their applications.

Because microcomputer technology changes so quickly, journal literature will be one of the best resources for basic information on current systems and software. Microcomputer Index provides citations to many of the most popular and easily obtainable journals on personal computers. IAC Magazine Index also contains references to a number of journals on microcomputers. For more of a focus on literature relating to the use of microcomputers in the library world, some particularly useful resources are *Computers in Libraries, Information Technology and Libraries*, and *Library Hi-Tech*. Citations to journal literature on microcomputer use in libraries can also be found in both *Library Literature* and *Library and Information Science Abstracts*. Once a decision has been made as to the type of computer system that will be purchased (a process covered in detail in Chapters 4 and 5), it will be helpful to look at journals that focus on that system. Most commonly used systems have spawned a field of magazines that address the hardware and software issues specific to that system.

The bibliography of basic computer reference materials contained in Appendix C includes a number of resources that can be valuable in providing a basic introduction to the terminology and concepts associated with microcomputers. It would be helpful for the manager to provide members of the planning team with copies of articles or books that have been particularly informative, or those that seem most applicable to your library environment. In this way, a consistent level of knowledge can be maintained among those staff members involved in the decision-making process.

Library visits

Visits to other libraries (as mentioned in the introduction to Section One) can be a particularly valuable method of collecting useful information about potential systems and applications. In addition, there may be opportunities for valuable collaboration with local libraries during the process of automation. Richard Anglin of the Ramapo Catskill Library System in Middletown, New York, wrote in *Library Journal*:

> This kind of cooperation can happen if the emphasis in the library's planning is on the ways to share staff training and reduce costs by cooperating with a neighbor who has similar work to do (not on the machinery and its capacity down to the last byte). Sharing can only take place if the machines chosen are compatible. That is why the staffs at cooperating libraries must talk together at the planning stage. The machines cannot be blamed if two libraries find their staffs using different machine languages, growing along lines dictated by the machines rather than those based on work to be performed and greater cooperation. The time for cooperation is in the

planning stages, before any equipment has been bought.[1]

Mr. Anglin's advice applies primarily to libraries which are part of a linked system; branches in a public or academic system, for example, or members of a cooperative network. In these cases, the possibility of building cooperative computer systems—for example, each library taking responsibility for developing one part of the system, from cataloging to circulation—is a great potential cost-saver, primarily in staff time and training. If a library is part of such a linked system, the manager should be sure to explore any opportunities for this type of cooperative automation process. The administrative offices for the system or network should be contacted to determine whether any projects of this sort have been attempted. If so, the manager should make inquiries to determine what the results of these efforts were. If not, it may make sense to talk with other library managers in the system to explore the possibilities for such a collaborative effort. The potential for increased savings and goodwill is enormous.

Libraries without these cooperative ties should still include library visits as a part of their planning process. A manager need not be planning a collaborative effort to benefit from this type of information gathering effort. The information gained from other library managers who have already faced similar questions and choices while automating their facilities can be an invaluable factor in the planning process. Talking with the staff and administration of libraries which have completed their own installations of microcomputer facilities can provide valuable insight into the particular issues that affect decision making in the process of evaluating, selecting, and installing equipment.

The more libraries visited, the more effective the planning process will be. If local libraries that have already successfully implemented microcomputer installations can be identified, those libraries are the top

---

[1]Anglin, Richard V. "Cooperate and plan before you buy anything: computer commandments." *Library Journal*, v. 109, Oct. 1, 1984: 1821-1822.

candidates for visits. There are a number of resources that can help in compiling of this list. Library associations can provide referrals to local microcomputer "success stories." Articles may have appeared in the library literature describing projects that have been implemented nearby; these articles may be located through a search of *Library Literature* or *Library and Information Science Abstracts*, in their print or online versions. Computer users groups and electronic bulletin boards may be helpful in locating other contacts. These organizations can also be excellent resources if there is interest in consulting with or visiting microcomputer managers in settings other than a traditional library environment.

Once the list has been assembled, the managers of these libraries (or offices) should be contacted to set up appointments for viewing their facilities; the reason for the visit should be explained, and the manager should be alerted to the type of information that is being sought. It may be possible to gain useful perspective not only on what techniques have been successful for them, but also on what they would do differently the next time. If possible, these site visits should be scheduled within a set period of time. No more than two to three weeks should be taken in this information gathering phase; scheduling the visits close together will make it possible to make more effective comparisons among the various sites while the information is still fresh in everyone's minds.

One thing to remember when discussing microcomputers with other users is that, more than nearly any other piece of equipment, a computer can inspire an extraordinary level of devotion from its users. Once members of a group have made the substantial investment of time and money in purchasing and learning a certain computer system, they have a vested interest in convincing themselves—and others—that their choice was flawless, and that no other system could have served their needs as effectively and efficiently. Take all claims of superior performance with a grain of salt, and draw conclusions based on what the computers in a library environment actually are accomplishing, and on how the employees in an automated library appear to feel about their work and the use of the computers in support of their activities. Remember, too, that what works well in one library environment may not be as successful in another setting. Find out what makes a particular system so attractive to the libraries visited; it may be that its appeal lies in its abilities to meet specific needs that do not exist in other library environments.

During each visit to other libraries and information centers, it is also possible to gather information on the vendors and distributors with whom these libraries have done business. Find out whether they contacted more than one vendor in their purchasing process, and if they have any complaints about (or compliments for) the one they settled on. It is in a library's best interest to work with a vendor that has already acquired a degree of familiarity with requirements and restrictions associated with library automation.

Planning and needs assessment

As mentioned in the introduction to this chapter, the planning process encompasses almost all of the issues discussed in this section of the book. In Chapter 3, the process of identifying a library's automation needs and translating those needs into specific goals and objectives for implementation is discussed in detail. The process of needs assessment is a vital part of the planning process, and must be undertaken early in the stages of any automation project.

When planning for automation, it is important to examine not only current needs and resources, but also the potential for expanded requirements over time. For example, the library which currently has little or no need for telecommunications capability may, at some point, wish to begin accessing online services from the library microcomputers. By making purchases that can accommodate future expansion, the facility manager can add to the base system already installed, and avoid some of the need to replace equipment when new needs arise.

The planning process must therefore include consideration of long-term library plans; future expansion or relocation may have an impact on the types of equipment and software purchased. Any plans for the library to become involved in cooperative efforts or networks may require that standardized equipment or software be purchased.

The rising importance of local area networks in the library environment does need to be considered in the planning and needs assessment process. Networks allow many users at separate workstations to access the same resources, ranging from large data files and CD-ROM databases to printers and modems. Since the networking of computers involves additional expenses for cabling and extra components, as well as specialized software programs, budget constraints can often prevent a library from including a network in its initial plans for automation. Even if a network will not be part of the original plan, it is still sensible to select microcomputers and software with the possibility of future networking in mind. Not all computers will operate with all forms of networks; it is well worth exploring the networking options currently available for any microcomputers, peripheral equipment, and software that you evaluate. More information on networking and other integration issues, can be found in Chapters 3 and 5.

Timetables

Each library needs to determine its own timetable for planning and implementing automation. It is important, however, to begin by establishing broad guidelines for the time spent in planning. These guidelines can later be altered as the planning progresses. By beginning with this structure, library managers and staff can avoid adopting unrealistic assumptions about the length of the process; any changes can likewise be made a part of a shared plan.

It is critical to put plans in writing, so as to effectively manage the schedule of a project as complex as selecting and installing an automated system. These timetables can be prepared by the manager alone, or by the planning team as a group effort. The advantage of involving the group in this exercise is that group members are less likely to feel as though arbitrary deadlines have been imposed upon them, and are more likely to feel a sense of commitment to finishing tasks by the dates agreed upon.

Documenting the plan

It is essential that all planning activities be fully documented. Without a written plan of action, much of the work that has gone into the information gathering process will be lost before the implementation of automation ever begins. The written plan, if presented effectively, will serve as a tool to procure financial support for the automation process, and will help staff members understand the direction in which the library is proceeding.

The written plan must cover several key points. First, a summary detailing the library's needs for automated tools. Next, a description of the planning process, including the composition of the planning team, and the activities undertaken by the team. Then, a brief discussion of the team's findings and recommendations. Finally, a breakdown of the costs associated with the proposed solution, and a timetable for purchase and implementation should be included. A sample outline for a planning document is included at the end of this chapter; it is only a guide, and may not include information pertinent to all library environments. It does, however, provide a starting point for those unfamiliar with the process of documenting automation activities. It is generally appropriate for the manager responsible for the automation project to write and submit this report; however, some managers find that a group writing project can be better suited to their library environments.

In addition to the formal plan for the introduction of microcomputers into the library, the documentation should include backup for the conclusions reached: notes from strategy sessions and site visits; product information from vendors; articles and reviews gathered from library andcomputer literature; and any other documents that have bearing on the plan itself. At least one member of the planning team should be responsible for maintaining and organizing this information.

One of the more effective ways of organizing the information is in a vertical file, with the information broken down into manageable categories. Categories can be determined "on-the-fly," by breaking general files into subfiles as information proliferates, or they can be defined before the information is acquired. If the second approach is taken, one source for file headings could be the chapter and topic headings in this book; most chapter titles can be used as general groupings, while subtitles within the chapters would be appropriate for folders within the main files.

Bringing the plan to life

When planning for an automated system is done effectively, the planning document provides a clear path to action for those involved in its implementation. A good plan takes into account the current *and* anticipated future needs of the library staff and patrons, the resources available for the automation project, and the projected impact of the technology on the library and its users. This is not an easy task, but it is an essential one. All these issues will confront library managers as they move into the world of library automation; those who have considered the issues *before* they become crises will be better prepared to address them.

The chapters that follow cover many of these aspects of planning for and managing microcomputer technology in the library. Needs assessment, cost analysis, comparison of systems and software, the installation process, and training topics are all addressed in this section of the book, and should be addressed in any plan for library automation. Any issues that affect the management of library automation should also be addressed in the planning for library automation; planning and management are inextricably entwined.

Sample Outline of Documentation

I. Executive summary

    A. Why does library need automation?

    B. What specific gains will be realized, and when?

    C. What is the timetable for the project?

II. The Planning Process

    A. Description of the planning team:

        1. Who was selected?

        2. What were the criteria for composition of team?

        3. What is the timetable for team activities?

    B. Methodology used

        1. Sources consulted (print, online, experts)

        2. Site visits made to other libraries and vendor showrooms.

III. Recommendations

    A. Projected applications of automated technology

        1. Management/clerical

        2. Library-specific

        3. Public access

    B. Recommended systems

    C. Timetable for implementation

IV. Financial information

    A. Anticipated expenses

    B. Potential funding sources.

Chapter 3

Needs Assessment

W hen library managers consider the issue of automation, the first question they must answer is "does our library require this technology?" In order to justify the substantial expenses involved in automation, the library manager must determine during the planning process whether computers will effectively meet the needs of the library's staff and patrons.

The book *Microcomputers for Library Decision Making: Issues, Trends, and Applications* contains an essay by Beverly L. Jones entitled, "Is a Microcomputer Really Necessary in Your Library Setting?" This essay examines the advantages and the disadvantages of microcomputers in libraries and concludes:

> Is a microcomputer necessary for your library environment? Yes, regardless of collection or budget size, or library type; the uses are limited largely by imagination. The trend toward increased use of microcomputers both in libraries and in society at large, may well combine to force any library to use a microcomputer. In so doing, a library enlarges its potential for resource and information sharing, sets the foundation for more effective and informed

decision making, and takes a potential big step toward
better serving its community of users.[2]

It is not enough, however, simply to know that the need for microcomputers exists. It is also necessary to know *where* and *why* that need
exists. Too many libraries buy computers before determining what those
computers will actually be expected to accomplish. Unfortunately, many
organizations attempt to use computers simply to automate tasks already
being done. Why is this a problem? Because the process of installing
automated systems gives us the opportunity to *rethink* the ways we
process information and perform tasks. The process of planning for
computer purchases is an opportunity to cast a critical eye over all our
operations, to identify workflow patterns and problems, and to find ways
to eliminate unnecessary tasks. Computers are ideally suited to the
performance of routine, repetitive tasks, and can thereby free staff
members for more creative and intellectual activities. If microcomputers
are used simply to replicate current routines, many advantages that
automated systems can bring to a library will not be gained. To avoid this
mistake, managers must carefully assess the needs of their staff and of
their patrons, and clarify the specific uses they envision for their computer
facilities.

Libraries face a unique challenge when considering the issues and
needs of automation, as they generally find themselves faced with diverse
uses for microcomputer technology. These needs can fall into any
combination of these three basic areas:

- The administrative needs of automating clerical, financial, and
  record-keeping functions;

- The library-specific needs of such activities as cataloging,
  acquisitions, and circulation; and

---

[2]*Microcomputers for library decision making: issues, trends, and applications.* Edited by
Peter Hernon and Charles R. McClure. Norwood, NJ, Ablex, 1986. Essay by Beverly L.
Jones, "Is a microcomputer really necessary in your library setting?" p. 3-17.

• The public access needs in those libraries choosing to provide microcomputers for patron use.

When a library first ventures into the arena of microcomputer use, it is often in an effort to facilitate the work of its staff members. Some libraries choose to begin with their management and clerical workload, using microcomputers for word processing, for database management, and for financial planning and bookkeeping. This type of automation is often referred to as "office automation," and information on the tools available for these tasks is available from a wide variety of sources; any bookstore is likely to have shelves overflowing with general and business-oriented texts on the use of microcomputer systems and software.

Other libraries make the decision to automate the administrative functions that are unique to the library environment—maintaining circulation records, recording library acquisitions, or creating an online system for entry and retrieval of catalog records. This type of automation is generally referred to as "library automation," and information on the related hardware components and software packages is available primarily from library-specific literature and organizations.

Although these two types of administrative activity are quite different in emphasis and impact, they are nonetheless closely linked. Computers can greatly improve the efficient use of time in both areas, and with proper planning, can also encourage the sharing of data and reduction of repetition. Budget planning on a computer spreadsheet can incorporate acquisitions and circulation data; databases used for clerical purposes can be linked to patron records contained in a circulation system; letters to vendors can include information from an acquisitions database. In order to maximize the effectiveness of a computer investment for these two forms of administrative use, each must be considered individually on the basis of its own needs; the needs for compatibility and data-sharing can then be evaluated in light of these primary requirements.

Once the automation of library activities has been accomplished—or, sometimes *before* it is accomplished—libraries may also find that the demand for public access computing facilities needs to be addressed. Public access microcomputers can be used for a variety of activities: accessing online databases; using CD-ROM-based information sources; even teaching computer literacy. However, the addition of public access microcomputers requires the careful consideration of available physical and human resources. A successful public access microcomputing facility in a library requires extensive planning.

This chapter is designed to help identify library automation needs and clarify them in the light of today's technology. It begins by defining each of the three basic categories of library automation needs, as well as the needs resulting from networking and other projects requiring integration and/or standardization of equipment and software. Once these needs have been grouped and defined, the process for identifying a library's specific needs is discussed.

Management and clerical needs

In the assessing of management and clerical needs, library managers can draw upon many of the tools used by managers in other types of office environments. Four applications areas offer vital tools for the administrative tasks associated with managing a library environment: word processing, spreadsheets, database management, and telecommunications.

Word processing is often one of the first computerized activities to be introduced into an office environment, and library offices are no exception to this trend. The use of word processing to replace most typing tasks can take an enormous burden of repetitive work from the shoulders of the support staff. Most libraries generate a vast array of form letters, ranging from notices of overdue materials to claims on missing serial issues. Word processing allows the staff to keep these forms available for easy customizing and printing, and eliminates the need to retype entire letters when making relatively small changes in the text. It also reduces the need for use of messy carbons for duplicate letters, as multiple copies of a single document can easily be printed. Its similarity to the traditional typing process makes it easier for staff to feel comfortable with the new technology, while the ease of revision, storage, and retrieval of documents will ensure that the technology will be appreciated by all who use it.

Financial planning and budgeting have in the past been managed primarily with pencil and paper spreadsheets and ledgers. Electronic spreadsheet programs make it possible to automate these activities, resulting in greatly improved error-checking, and providing the capacity for instantaneous recalculation of financial documents. Spreadsheet programs are an invaluable tool for managers involved in any aspect of financial record-keeping or planning.

Database management programs allow users to maintain inventories, mailing lists, and other records of information that in the past have taken up substantial space in paper format. They also speed the process of making across-the-board changes to the format or content of individual records in a collection of information. Everything from patron lists to equipment inventories can be maintained in database files, allowing easy access to specific information within the files, and a wide range of reporting options.

Finally, telecommunications software provides the capacity to connect to a multitude of outside resources. A few of the applications of these programs in the library office environment are: the transfer of documents to outside locations, ranging from other libraries to administrative offices; connection to outside databases for retrieving information; and connection to in-house resources such as mini- or mainframe computers for retrieval of centralized administrative information or use of institutional electronic mail facilities.

These are only a few of the many uses that library managers and their staffs can make of current microcomputer technology in their regular activity. As new application programs become available, these management activities are likely to expand to take advantage of the new technologies.

In order to effectively determine requirements for the automation of these managerial and clerical functions, it is necessary to carefully define the scope of activities involved in the administration of the library. The type, volume, and scheduling of written documents—including correspondence, newsletters, and reports—should be measured, to determine the features necessary in a word processing program. The budgeting process and responsibilities should be laid out, so as to assess needs for spreadsheeting capabilities. The information being collected and analyzed or referenced regularly should be examined, so that potential uses for database management programs can be specified, and suitable software chosen. And telecommunications needs, ranging from the searching of online databases for administrative purposes to the transferring of files and information to and from other libraries and institutions, should be identified so that appropriate software and hardware can be purchased.

Library automation needs

In some ways, developments in the field of library automation mirror those in office automation; both fields focus on the automation of repetitious tasks, in order to free staff for activities requiring more judgement and skill. In other ways, the library automation field is completely different from that of office automation; whereas the latter is found in any number of varied office environments using every conceivable type of computer system, the former is found exclusively in the library environment, and its more specialized nature and clientele constrains it to a far smaller range of available systems and programs.

Library automation can be implemented on a relatively small scale using microcomputers, or on a larger scale, using mini- and mainframe computers. In larger academic and public library systems, microcomputers are generally not powerful enough to store the huge databases of information associated with the cataloging and circulation of material. This book does not address the issues involved in non-microcomputer library automation, but focuses instead on the issues facing smaller libraries and information centers wishing to automate library functions through the use of microcomputer systems and software.

The primary areas of library function in which automation is usually implemented are cataloging (including the creation of online public access catalogs), interlibrary loan, circulation systems, and acquisitions systems. These functions can be automated one at a time, allowing for gradual integration of microcomputer-based activities, or through multi-function software packages, which ensure the smooth integration of related tasks among the functional areas.

A library's individual requirements for automation of library functions will depend upon a number of outside factors. Here, more than in any other area, it is imperative that libraries attempt to work cooperatively with each other. Libraries within public or academic systems, and those belonging to cooperative organizations, will have a particular responsibility to automate their records and transactions in such a way as to allow the sharing of data with their affiliated libraries. This is particularly true in the areas of cataloging and interlibrary loan. If microcomputers are already in use within the organization, the type of systems installed will have a substantial effect upon the availability of software programs for library automation. The issues of compatibility and integration are addressed in more detail in the section of this chapter entitled, "Networking and compatibility needs."

In order to successfully automate library functions, it is most important to define requirements that accurately reflect the activities and needs of the library staff performing the tasks. Cataloging systems that do not allow input or output of records in the format used by the library will create an enormous and probably unnecessary set of additional conversion tasks. The compatibility of library automation programs with current methods of cataloging, logging in acquisitions, and recording patron and circulation data is vital to the smooth implementation of automated systems for both staff and patrons.

Public access needs

As microcomputers have become more common as standard tools in both schools and businesses, an entirely new medium for information dissemination has grown up around them. An increasing number of publishers are now distributing information that was once available only in print in "machine-readable" formats. These new types of publications include: software packages, such as educational games and employee tutorials; data diskettes, ranging from magazines on computer disk to disks of specialized statistical data; and the rapidly expanding area of CD-ROM, a medium which allows microcomputers to access huge quantities of information from a specialized compact disc format. In addition, online databases which can be accessed only through microcomputers or terminals are becoming an increasingly important reference tool in many libraries.

The role of libraries as disseminators of information has naturally led to the inclusion of microcomputers in libraries for use by the public in exploring this new field of information publishing. Microcomputers equipped with modems can be used to access a vast number of online databases; this type of information searching can be done by the reference librarian or the library patron. Although the cost of providing this type of public access service can be prohibitive, the potential exists for vast expansion of the library's range of information sources. The addition of a CD-ROM drive creates additional opportunities for libraries to provide patrons with access to more information in a more usable manner; again, although the costs can be high, a strong case can be made for the value of providing this type of resource.

The availability of computer-based information sources is not, however, the only rationale for providing public access microcomputer facilities. Indeed, many libraries with public access computers do not use those computers for access to online or CD-ROM databases. There is a growing need in today's workplace for "computer-literate" employees. Libraries have the opportunity to expand their traditional roles in combatting illiteracy by making public access computers available to their patrons. Just as the library has always provided access to books, journals, and other information resources that individuals could not afford to purchase for themselves, so the library can also provide access to computer equipment and software.

There are a number of issues that must be addressed before a public access microcomputer facility can be implemented in a library environment. Among the questions that must be asked are:

- •What funding sources are available, not only for the startup equipment costs, but also for the ongoing costs of staff training, collection development, and equipment upkeep?

•What forms of instruction, if any, will be offered to patrons by the library? Will a course on computing fundamentals, or demonstration of skills be required for use of the equipment, and if so, what responsibility does the library have to provide patrons with basic instruction?

•What software will be needed for use with the computers, and how many copies of each program should be purchased?

•Will software be allowed to circulate outside of the library? If so, how will copyright and data security risks be protected against?

•How will computer resources be cataloged and stored?

•Will access to online and/or CD-ROM databases be available on these computers?

•If the computers will be used to access online databases or bulletin board services, what telecommunications capacity will be needed?

•Will the computers be networked together in order to share peripheral equipment and resources (such as printers, CD-ROM drives, and central copies of software)? If so, how will software use and the placement of peripheral equipment be affected?

•Will new staff positions be necessary, or will current staff be trained in microcomputer skills?

•What, if any, relationship will exist between the public access microcomputing center and other computing activities in the library? Will they share staff? Software? Peripheral devices?

The above questions only scratch the surface of the public access microcomputing topic. Those interested in exploring the issues more fully have a variety of resources available to them. Several fine books have dealt specifically with the issues related to implementing public access microcomputing in libraries; among them are *Public Access Microcomputers in Academic Libraries* (Chicago, American Library Association, 1987), *Developing Microcomputer Work Areas in Academic*

Libraries (Westport, Meckler, 1988), and *Public Access CD-ROMs in Libraries: Case Studies* (Westport, Meckler, 1990).

Networking and compatibility needs

In today's library environment, it is not unusual to see computer equipment from a wide range of vendors connected together. Local area networks allow microcomputers to share information and equipment even when the micros themselves use incompatible file formats; communications technology can allow the microcomputers to share that same information and equipment with minicomputers and even with mainframes.

This trend toward communication among computers must be taken into account when assessing the automation needs of a library. Although connectivity has its price, in the form of hardware, software, installation, and management costs, it also has the potential to save substantial amounts of money. Data communication devices can reduce equipment costs by allowing the shared use of expensive peripheral equipment like printers, scanners, and modems. They can also improve productivity by allowing more efficient transfer of data among employees.

In the needs assessment process, there are several factors that must be considered in relation to networking and integration. Is there existing computer equipment—peripheral devices, mini- or mainframe computers, even software—that will need to be used with a new microcomputer system? If so, this requirement must be clearly documented and considered in the evaluation of available systems. Is there a need for employees to share peripheral devices? If so, to what extent?

The issues of standardization and compatible data formats are particularly important when the area of the library to be automated is one dealing with bibliographic data. Most of the currently used standard formats for this type of data are based upon the MARC record standard. Libraries that plan to use their computers to access data from a cooperative cataloging source such as OCLC or RLIN will need to ensure that their equipment and software is capable of working with data in the proper formats.

Those libraries interested in the networking of their computers have a wide variety of information sources available to them. There are references to a number of useful journals, articles, and books on the topic in the bibliography in Appendix B. However, the lightning-fast changes in LAN technology make it nearly impossible to obtain up-to-date information in print. The best sources for information on local area networking and how it may apply to a library's needs are other librarians and microcomputer managers, contacted through the computer users groups and library organizations mentioned in Chapter 2.

The primary issue to consider in networking and integration is to what degree the library's computers will be used to share data and/or equipment with other computers, whether those other computers are in the library as well, or in other locations. Academic libraries may need to connect their computers to a campus-wide network; corporate libraries may wish to access mainframe resources through their microcomputers; small libraries may be forced to share limited peripheral resources like printers and CD-ROM drives through networking. In the planning process, communications and compatibility needs should be identified, so that they can be factored into the choices of hardware, software, and communications equipment for the library.

Needs assessment process

A needs assessment process, in the broadest terms, consists of identifying goals and objectives for a project, and identifying requirements for its successful completion. In the case of implementing microcomputer technology, the identification of goals and objectives is directly related to the broad categories of library automation defined in this chapter. Library managers must first determine what type of automation they wish to pursue: the automation of clerical activities, the automation of professional library activities, or the provision of public access facilities for patrons.

Once the broad outlines of automation goals have been identified, it will be necessary to outline the more specific objectives that the library hopes to accomplish through the installation and use of microcomputers. One example of the relationship of goals to objectives would be the following: a public library might define one of its automation goals to be the provision of public access microcomputer services to its patrons, with the specific objectives being the installation of three microcomputers and a library of popular educational and business software packages, and the provision of basic computer training. To determine a library's specific automation goals and objectives, the planning team will need to carefully examine current activities, looking first for areas where repetitious tasks, duplication of effort, or tedious paperwork could be replaced by automated processes, and then for additional services that could be made available to library patrons.

A daily log of activities for all professional employees can provide a starting point for analyzing workflow. Using these logs the planning team can construct a simple flow chart of daily activities, and can then determine where automation could save time or alter workflow to improve effectiveness. It is important to specifically examine the library's potential needs in each the broad categories discussed above (management, library-specific, public access, and networking and integration); one of the best ways to gather this information is by recording information about time spent on tasks and other workflow information. The information gathered in this needs assessment can then be analyzed and included in the overall plan for library automation, and will form the broad outlines of the library's system requirements.

Chapter 4

System Requirements

Once automation needs have been specified in terms of goals and objectives, definition of potential system requirements can begin. In order to complete this task, it is necessary to both understand the system requirements document, and identify the available resources.

This chapter begins with a discussion of the types of resources that are necessary in the installation and maintenance of an automated system in a library environment. Before the planning team can define requirements for new equipment and staff, it must first identify the physical and human resources already available to the library. By examining these resources, the team should determine both what is currently available, and what potential there is for expansion to support a new automated system. In addition, the team must identify the available financial resources, which are the major constraint in defining new equipment and staffing requirements.

Once the available resources have been identified and categorized, the team can begin to specify new requirements. The system requirements document translates broad objectives into specific equipment, staffing, and financial requirements. The information already gathered on available resources guides this process by defining the boundaries of realistic action.

Identification of available resources

The first resource area to be explored is that of financial resources. Without funding, a venture into automation is nearly impossible. Even when donated equipment is available, the costs of maintaining a microcomputer installation must considered from the start. Although this chapter does consider the impact of financial resources on the system requirements process, more in-depth information on the cost/benefit analysis that must be undertaken in automation planning is contained in Chapter 6.

It is not only the available funding, however, that determines what systems can realistically be implemented. There are two other resources that figure into the planning process; physical resources, which range from available space to already installed computer equipment, and human resources, which encompass the library staff and the support personnel available to the library through associated branches of an institution or company. Each of these areas is covered in more detail in the following sections.

Physical resources

Before specifications can be written for new equipment, two aspects of current physical resources need to be considered. First, the space available for the proposed system must be identified, and its suitability for housing computer equipment must be assessed. For systems designed to automate management and/or library-specific functions, the team is less likely to need to identify new areas; instead, an analysis of current space and how it is utilized will be necessary. Do those employees who would receive workstations have space available on their desks for the equipment? If not, is there sufficient floor space for the addition of computer tables? If desk and table space is at a premium, equipment with a small "footprint" (the square footage the equipment occupies on a desktop) should be emphasized in the system requirements.

When a public access installation is being considered, space takes on even more significance. The area being considered must have sufficient space available to house appropriate tables or desks, and must provide for secure access to the equipment and software as well. Microcomputer equipment and software is expensive, attractive, and easily stolen; the space chosen for any public access microcomputer installation must take that into consideration. A library staff member should be able to monitor everyone entering and exiting the microcomputer area, and no building exits should be adjacent to the microcomputer work area.

Whether the computers will be used for internal use or for public access activities, the quality of the electrical wiring, and the electrical system's ability to carry the additional load of the computers and peripheral devices must be examined. Along the same lines, environmental factors such as humidity and dust should be considered; most microcomputer installations function most reliably in an air-conditioned environment. If the space being considered is not already air-conditioned, the possibility of installing this feature should be considered. More information on these types of environmental concerns can be found in the second section of this book, in Chapter 11, which deals with preventive maintenance issues.

Another aspect of current physical resources that should be considered in this phase of the team's research is the availability of existing equipment. If the library is replacing an obsolete system, some equipment may be salvageable for use in a new system. In addition, some items that are not commonly considered as computer equipment can be pressed into service as components of an automated system. Some electronic typewriters, for instance, can be used as printers with a microcomputer system. All current equipment, ranging from power strips through currently used computers and printers, should be inventoried and their potential for use in a new system should be considered.

Human resources

All too often, the planning process for a new microcomputer installation neglects to consider the issue of human resources. Once an automated system has been installed, it will only be useful if it is maintained by trained staff members. This is true not only for public access machines, but also for administrative and library-specific computers. Without a computer-literate staff whose duties specifically include the upkeep of the computer system, the project is likely to end in failure. In assessing current resources, the team should find out whether any library staff members have an interest in and familiarity with computers, as well as whether current workloads will permit any staff members to take on the added responsibility of regularly monitoring the microcomputer installation. If not, the availablility of employees elsewhere in the institution or company who can assist in this activity— for instance, a computer support group for a company or university, or media aides at a school library—should be investigated. These are important resources to identify and include in any systems planning.

Financial resources

The primary financial resource that must be considered in preparation for defining system requirements is, of course, the budget for the automation project. Without a commitment on the part of the library's management to fund a microcomputer installation, the system cannot be defined or implemented. However, the cost of the equipment and software is only a portion of the overall cost of installing a computerized facility. The financial resources allocated for the project must cover all the costs that will be associated with the system and its maintenance. It is essential that a full cost/benefit analysis be performed in the planning process; one that will take into account not only the many costs involved, but also the tangible *and* intangible benefits to patrons and staff that will result from the implementation of an automated system.

In some ways, the process of securing financial resources for an automation project can be a catch-22; without first defining the requirements for a system, it is difficult to assess the costs and benefits of installing it. However, without knowing the funding that will be available for a project, it is difficult to specify the requirements. Because this book is addressed primarily to the first-time planner of a microcomputer facility, the topic of system evaluation (Chapter 5) is considered before that of cost/benefit analysis (Chapter 6). This is to provide the planner with a general understanding of the necessary components of a microcomputer system. Those planners who are able to estimate approximate costs of a system may wish to reverse the order of these activities.

Definition of requirements

The definition of a library's system requirements begins with the needs assessment process covered in Chapter 3. The goals and objectives for automation that were identified in that process must now be translated into specific requirements for an automated system. The requirements can be broken down into three major components:

- •First, the system objectives, which succinctly restate the information gathered in the needs assessment process;

- •Second, the equipment requirements, which broadly outline the type and scope of automated system being considered; and

- •Third, the financial requirements, which define the funds available for the purchase of equipment and support of the system.

Each of these components is considered separately below.

System objectives

In completing a thorough needs assessment process, the planning team should already have gathered the basic components of the library's system objectives. Using this information, the team must now translate the library's needs into specific objectives for the new microcomputer system.

It is crucial to remember in this process that objectives must be clearly defined and quantifiable goals, rather than general statements of need. Thus, if a need to produce documents more efficiently has been identified, that need should be translated into a system objective such as provision of word processing services that can meet the library's specific documentation needs. Another example would be the translation of a need for automated circulation support into an objective that the system be able to provide "online" information about availability of library materials, generate overdue notices, and calculate fines.

In both of the above examples, the library's needs for improved services in a given area have been translated into standards that a given system must meet in order to be considered for purchase. In each area where automation needs have been identified, these needs should be stated as requirements.

Equipment requirements

Although many equipment requirements will emerge in the system requirements process, there may be some that should be identified separately. Some issues that should be stated in any requirements documentation are the acceptable size of the equipment to be purchased, the environment in which the equipment must be able to operate, and any special requirements that may be necessary to meet the specialized needs of handicapped staff and/or patrons.

These specific requirements should be clearly defined and communicated to vendors. Any equipment that the team has seen on visits to other libraries or other sites that were notably attractive or unacceptable should be included in the definition of requirements at this point.

Financial requirements

As mentioned above, it is often difficult to clearly state the financial requirements for the system before initial prices for systems meeting the other requirements have been determined. However, it is crucial to begin with a working figure, even if the figure has no concrete base in a committed budget. Before the library can approach vendors for systems, the library's representatives must have a general idea of the amount of money they are willing to spend, both for the initial investment and for continued upkeep.

This last point is of particular importance. It is not enough to be able to purchase the equipment and software at the outset of the automation process. It is also necessary for the library to make a commitment to the maintenance, training, upgrades, and other ongoing expenses associated with the installation of any computer-based system. In Chapter 6, the costs (and benefits) of a microcomputer system are discussed in more detail, providing the planning team with a base on which to make decisions about financial requirements.

Documentation of requirements

Once this process of stating needs as requirements has been completed, the resulting information can be compiled into a single document, and broken down into more functional areas. Some categories to include in a systems requirements document might include:

1) Current and expansion capacity: If the library's needs grow, will the system be able to handle the expanded requirements for data storage with its current components? If not, can it be upgraded, or would it need to be replaced with a new system? If the need for additional workstations arises, can the system accommodate the additional workload? Will the system run a full range of software, above and beyond the immediately specified applications? The potential expansion needs should be defined as clearly as possible, with an emphasis on providing room for expansion as new needs are identified. A system that meets only a library's current needs and cannot be expanded as the library's needs and expectations grow should not be considered.

2) Physical aspects of components: If the system and/or display unit(s) need to fit in a specific room, or on a specific size desk or table, the size and/or weight requirements should be specified. In addition, the environment that the system will be housed in should be fully described, so that the special power or air quality needs of a proposed system can be considered in light of the available space.

3) Ease of use: The training aids needed—classroom training, computer-based training, book and/or cassette-based tutorials—should be specified, as should the expected time it will take to have library staff trained to a level that makes the system a useful tool.

4) Available applications software: The range of applications necessary should be a natural outgrowth of the needs assessment process. In the administrative area, word processing, database management, spreadsheet, and telecommunications tools should all be specified as

needed. In the area of library-specific automation, those areas to be automated should be clearly spelled out—circulation? cataloging? acquisitions?—and any interaction necessary among the functions should also be specified. For patrons, the types of educational, recreational, and/or business-oriented software required for the system should be listed.

5) Reporting capability: Any information that users will require the system to generate should be described as specifically as possible. What types of printed output will be needed? What information should be obtainable through interactive queries at a display terminal? How should the information be organized in printed or displayed reports? These questions are particularly important in the area of library-specific automation, where packages are often less flexible.

Chapter 5

System Evaluation

Once the process of determining library needs and identifying available resources has been completed, the evaluation of available systems can begin. This activity can draw heavily upon planning activities already completed, in particular any reviews of current microcomputer and library automation literature, as well as information gathered from visits to other libraries. With that data as a starting point, the planning team can turn its attention to a more in-depth review of available microcomputer systems, and their appropriateness for the library's specific needs.

In addition to seeing technology in use at other library sites, team members should consult with computer vendors to determine what technologies are currently available for purchase, and to get a general sense of equipment and software costs. This information can be gathered by telephone and written requests for product information, as well as by visits to computer stores.

Armed with this information, the group can identify local vendors carrying systems that may meet the library's automation needs. This is not the time to make commitments to dealers, or even to discuss pricing structures. The visits should be purely informational, an effort at gathering technical information on currently available products. This information can be filed by vendor or by product, for future reference when a firmer plan for library automation has been formulated.

The sections below provide an overview of the key components of microcomputer-based systems; this information can be used as a starting point when considering key system factors. They also serve as a brief introduction to current microcomputer technology. The difficulty in providing this type of specific system information in a published book is the likelihood that it will be outdated before the book ever finds its way into the hands of interested readers. Much of what is discussed here is general enough to provide a base to which information gathered through recent journal articles and visits to vendors can be added.

This book is unusual in that it covers the process of system evaluation before that of cost/benefit analysis; not all libraries will wish to follow this model. I have chosen to cover system evaluation first because it provides a basis for the novice microcomputer user to make intelligent decisions about necessary funding for a proposed project. However, those users who are familiar with the pricing of microcomputer equipment and the services associated with maintaining a microcomputer facility may be better served by completing the cost/benefit analysis before the evaluation of specific systems begins—this will enable them to limit their evaluation to those systems which they know will fall within their price range.

Microcomputer components

The logical starting point for a discussion of system requirements is the computer itself. Microcomputers are made up of a number of elements, however, making the choice of a specific system and configuration far more complex. The primary components of most microcomputers are described below; the role and importance of each component, its relationship to performance, and its effect on system cost are discussed. The focus of these descriptions is on Apple Macintosh and IBM compatible microcomputers; because these two types of systems are most prevalent in academic and business computing, even those school and public libraries which have until now used other computer systems (for example, Apple][s) are beginning to shift to these two in order to give their users access to standardized systems.

Processor chip

The processor, also known as the (Central Processing Unit), is the heart of the microcomputer. In the IBM-compatible and Macintosh worlds, the processor upon which the computer is based is a major feature of the computer's speed and power, and is often featured prominently in discussions of or advertisements for the unit.

The two factors influencing processor chip performance are the number of bits in the interface, and the clock speed at which the chip processes instructions.

IBM-compatible

In IBM-compatible systems, the processor is one of a series of microprocessor chips manufactured by Intel Corporation. This series begins with the 8086 and 8088 chips, which are used in the original IBM-PC and PC/XT. These chips have an 8-bit interface, and are limited to clock speeds ranging from 4.77 mhz to 10 mhz. The next chip in this series is the 80286, a 16-bit chip used as the basis for the IBM-AT and compatible machines; this chip has a clock speed ranging from 8 mhz to 20 mhz. The 286 was followed by two similar chips; the 80386 and 80386SX. Both of these chips are based on 32-bit technology; however, the SX version is limited to a 16-bit transfer of information. The 386 chip can run at speeds up to 33 mhz; the 386SX is limited to a speed of 16 mhz. At this writing, 80486-based microcomputers are beginning to appear on the market, but are not widely available.

Macintosh

In the Macintosh family of computers, the processors are manufactured by Motorola. The original Macintosh, Macintosh 512 and 512E, the Macintosh Plus, and the Macintosh SE are all based upon the Motorola 68000 chip, which has a 32-bit bus. The Macintosh II, which is no longer manufactured but can still be purchased from dealer stock or as second-hand material, is based upon the 68020 chip. The most recent line of Macintosh computers, including the Macintosh IIx, IIcx, IIci, and SE/30, are all based upon the 68030 chip, which also has a 32-bit bus.

Co-processor chip

In IBM-compatible and Macintosh computers, it is possible to enhance the speed and efficiency of certain operations by installing additional processing chips. The most common of these chips are called math co-processors, and they can greatly speed the completion of mathematical calculations in application programs such as spreadsheets, databases, and statistical analysis packages. If a microcomputer is being purchased for use with calculation-intensive applications, the purchase of a math co-processor chip should be considered. However, if the computer will be used primarily for character-based activities such as word-processing or telecommunications, it is less likely that such an addition would result in noticeable system improvements.

Memory

The amount of internal memory that a microcomputer contains refers to its RAM, or random access memory. This is the work area that the computer uses to store programs and/or data that are currently in use. Most RAM is volatile memory, meaning that when the computer's power is turned off, all information stored in RAM is lost. Some laptop computers use nonvolatile RAM, which ensures that even in the case of battery failure, important data that has been retrieved into memory will not be lost. Random access memory should not be confused with disk storage space, although both are often described in terms of megabytes of capacity.

IBM-compatible

In the IBM-compatible line of computers, basic memory is generally added in units of 128 kilobytes, ranging from a low of 256K to a high of 640K. Until recently, the MS-DOS operating system used by most IBM-compatible computers prevented the access of any memory beyond the 640K barrier. It is now possible, however, to access memory beyond 640K using a variety of methods, ranging from DOS software utilities to new operating systems like OS/2 and Presentation Manager. In fact, the growing memory requirements of many application programs, most notably local area network programs, can result in an immediate need for memory in amounts greater than 640K. Before specifying memory requirements for an IBM-compatible system, it is essential that the range of applications likely to be run on that system be considered, and that the vendors of those applications be contacted regarding specific memory requirements.

Macintosh

In the Macintosh line, the current low-end machine, the Macintosh Plus, comes with one megabyte of memory, expandable to 4MB. The Plus, and the earlier Macintosh models like the 128K, 512K, and 512Ke use memory in 256KB chips. In the higher-level Macintosh machines, memory can be expanded to a high of 16MB using 1MB memory chips. No operating system modifications are necessary for the Macintosh and its applications to utilize this additional memory capacity.

Display

The choice of a display monitor is critical to the acceptance of the computer by new users. If the monitor does not provide a clear and readable display, or if it cannot display the graphics or character sets the user requires, the computer will not be a useful tool.

IBM-compatible

In the IBM-compatible line of microcomputers, the range of display types can be overwhelming to new buyer. Those users interested only in monochrome displays must determine the basic color wanted (green on black, amber on black, or black on white), and whether or not graphics will be required. If graphics are required—and they often are, if only to display basic graphs and charts—the decision of Hercules-compatible vs. VGA-quality monochrome graphics adaptors becomes an issue. A good basic choice for a monochrome display is a green or amber on black display with a Hercules-compatible graphics adaptor. If very high-quality resolution is desired on a monochrome screen, a VGA monochrome graphics adapter can be installed. Those interested in high-quality displays for desktop publishing applications may need a monochrome monitor capable of displaying multiple shades of gray for shading purposes; these applications demand a gray-scale monitor and compatible adaptor card.

If color is required on an IBM-compatible system, the range of choices widens still further. The most basic color display available uses a CGA, or color graphics adaptor, card and monitor. The next step up, with better resolution, is EGA, or extended graphics adaptor. Following EGA is VGA color. The VGA (video graphics adaptor) standard is not yet firmly established, and variations on VGA emerge on a regular basis; if high-quality, high-resolution color graphics are required, recent journal articles and local vendors should be consulted as to options and costs.

Macintosh

With Macintosh computers, the basic models of the Plus and SE provide no immediate options; the built-in monitor is black on white, using high-resolution graphics. With Macintosh II and above, it is necessary to purchase a monitor, and then many of the same questions mentioned above for IBM compatible systems need to be asked: If the display will be monochrome, must it display high-quality gray-scale images? If it will be color, what quality of resolution will be required? The size, too, should be considered. Desktop publishing applications usually demand a monitor which will display at least one full-sized 8-1/2 x 11 inch page; some applications require that two facing pages be displayed.

When considering a monitor for desktop publishing applications, it is also important to determine whether the monitor provides a true WYSIWYG (what you see is what you get) display to the user. In environments where precise placing of text and graphics is important, this can be an important feature.

Some additional issues to consider in monitor selection include the availability of input devices for the screen. Some monitors provide touch-screen or light-pen capacity, allowing users to select items from the screen using their finger or a special light-pen. One important consideration with touch-screen monitors in a public-access environment will be any special cleaning routines and supplies that the monitor will require.

Input devices

The touch screens and light-pen devices mentioned briefly above are examples of input devices; components of the system that allow the users to communicate information to the computer's processor. They are not, however, the most common of these devices. Described below are some other system components that will need to be evaluated for inclusion in a new system. In addition to these items, the computer's storage units are also a form of input device, but are discussed in more detail in the next section.

The most obvious and common input device on the computer is the keyboard, used to enter character-based commands. Although many computers do come with a standard keyboard, most IBM-compatible and Macintosh computers also allow the user to purchase and add on a variety of third-party keyboards. Some things to consider when evaluating a keyboard are:

- The size of the keyboard;

- The layout of the keys (are the Enter and Shift keys conveniently placed? what about other special purpose keys?);

- The tactile response of the keys when pressed;

- The "clicks," or noise the keyboard makes when they keys are pressed; and

- The availability of programmable function keys.

Another input device that is a standard component of Macintosh systems, and is becoming increasingly common on IBM compatible systems, is the mouse. This is a pointing device that allows the user to move the cursor around on the screen. It has one or more buttons allowing the selection of options from the screen, as well. The mouse is particularly useful with graphically based operating systems (commonly referred to as GUIs, or Graphical User Interfaces), and in programs that include manipulation of graphic images. This type of input can also be obtained using a trackball, which allows the user to rotate a ball set into a flat surface, or a joystick, which involves the manipulation of a protruding stick, in order to move the cursor on the screen.

Other items that serve similar input purposes are scanners, digitizers, and bar wand devices. These are discussed in more detail in the section of the chapter dealing with peripheral equipment.

Storage devices

All microcomputers need to store information on, and retrieve it from, some sort of media. The most common form of storage in the microcomputer world is the floppy disk, a magnetically coated disk upon which the computer records digital information. When microcomputers were first introduced, the standard magnetic floppy disk size was 5-1/4", and this format is still used in many IBM-compatible microcomputers. The introduction of the Macintosh, which uses 3-1/2" diskettes in a harder plastic cover, has spurred the greater adoption of this format, and most laptop computers, as well as the newer line of IBMs and compatibles, use this 3-1/2" format.

Low density (referred to as dual density) 5-1/4" diskettes can store 360K of information on them; high density 5-1/4" diskettes can hold up to 1.2MB of data. Low density single-sided 3-1/2" diskettes can hold up to 400K of data; low density double-sided 3-1/2" diskettes can hold up to 1MB of data; and high-density 3-1/2" diskettes can hold up to 1.44MB of data. The total formatted capacity of a given diskette will vary, based upon the type of computer and disk drive used to format the diskette.

Floppy drives are only one type of magnetic disk storage, however. Hard drives (also known as fixed disk drives or Winchester drives) also store information on magnetically coated disks. These disk drives, however, can store much higher capacities of information, ranging from 10MB of data up to hundreds of megabytes. Although a hard drive is much more useful for storing programs and data to be used at a single machine, a floppy disk drive is also necessary for the transfer of data to other machines, and the loading of application programs.

There are other forms of data storage available for microcomputers, and several of these are discussed in the section of this chapter dealing with peripheral equipment.

Communication ports

Microcomputers can use a variety of methods to communicate with peripheral equipment and other computers. It is important to find out what options for communication any given system has, and whether these can be used or adapted for the planned applications within the library.

One of the most common communication standards is that of serial communication, which can be implemented in a variety of ways. On IBM compatible computers, serial communications take place over RS-232 type cables and connectors. Most IBM-compatible microcomputers have either one or two built-in serial ports. The early IBM PCs, XTs, and compatibles had 25-pin serial ports, while the IBM ATs and compatibles have 9-pin serial ports. On the Macintosh, serial communications are possible through the printer and modem ports on the back of the computer, which are din-8 ports.

Serial ports are used for data communications over modems, in connections to other computers, and for connection to printers and other peripherals with serial connections. Serial ports can also be used for connection to some networks and printer sharing devices.

On most IBM-compatible computers, parallel communication ports are also standard equipment. Parallel ports are used to connect primarily to printers, and to some other peripheral devices. Although parallel connections are often simpler to set up, and can communicate some types of information (for example, data to a printer), they are limited by the distances they can span.

Macintosh computers do not use parallel interfaces, but they do come with a standard SCSI (small computer system interface) port. This port can be used to connect storage devices and a wide range of peripheral devices. One advantage of SCSI devices is that they can be daisy-chained together, allowing several peripherals to share a single port on the computer. They also provide for higher-speed data transfer than many other types of connection. SCSI ports can be added to IBM-compatible computers, but are not as common in those configurations.

Expandability

Although a particular machine may meet all of a given institution's current needs for processing and storage, it is always possible that those needs will grow and change. As part of the system evaluation process, it is important to examine a computer's capacity for later expansion. There are several factors that contribute to this evaluation:

- First, can the computer's RAM (memory) be expanded at a later date? As application programs begin to require more and more memory to function properly, this issue is becoming increasingly important;

- Second, is it compatible with a range of additional data storage options, including larger, faster hard drives and optical disk units?

- Third, can the display be upgraded if additional graphics capability is needed?

- Fourth, are there expansion slots in the computer allowing for the addition of processing boards and boards required by peripheral equipment?

- Fifth, what kind of compatibility with peripheral equipment exists? If additional printers, scanners, modems, or other equipment become necessary, will the system unit be able to support these items?

Software base

The range of application programs available for the systems being evaluated is a critical issue. With the Macintosh and IBM compatible families of computers, it is likely that most application needs can be met by available software. However, even with these standard systems, if the organization has specialized needs, particularly those geared toward library automation, the availability of appropriate software will be a primary factor in the selection of a system. Planners should be wary of software publishers promising an imminent release of their program for a new operating environment; until the software has been seen running on the system in question in a commercially available form—not just a demo—it is risky to base plans for the computer system on the expected availability of the program. "Vaporware," a program that is announced by the manufacturer and never released, is not an unusual phenonmenon in the software publishing industry.

Reliability

Reliability of equipment is something all users expect when they purchase a computer system; however, not all users end up with reliable systems. It is important to investigate the reliability of any system being considered. This can be done by reviewing literature on the system from microcomputer journals (see the list of of current journals in Appendix C), or by contacting users of the system to inquire how many repairs they have needed on their computers. Vendors will generally provide prospective customers with a list of system users; the members of users groups are also good sources of information on system reliability.

Compatibility

The issue of compatibility is always important when a library considers purchasing of microcomputer equipment. There are three primary areas in which libraries must consider compatibility needs: within the larger organization, within the library world, and within the patron's frame of reference.

In their own institutional environment, libraries may need to purchase equipment using compatible operating systems. If the larger organization in which the library exists within has strictly IBM compatible, MS-DOS based machines, the library may need to purchase similar systems to ensure that programs and data can be shared easily with other units. If the organization is networked, it may only be necessary for the systems to have the capacity to connect to the existing local or wide area network; the range of suitable systems can vary, depending upon the network in question.

In the library world, there are two issues for compatibility. First, there are the compatibility needs dictated by any standard for processing and storage of data. If the library needs to use a particular system for library-related data processing (the library-specific needs discussed in Chapter 3), this requirement will play a major role in determining what hardware system can be used. The other issue for library compatibility is the degree to which the library plans to use such bibliographic utilities as OCLC and RLIN. Libraries planning to use their automated systems to access data from bibliographic utilities should consult with the technical support personnel at those utilities to obtain any specific system requirements.

Libraries installing public access computers will need to consider their patrons' computing environment and needs when selecting systems. If the library plans to provide computers as an extension to the computer education programs in local school systems, the prevalence of Apple II computers in primary and secondary schools may mean that similar systems will best meet the needs of the children at these schools, as well as their parents. However, if the motivation for the public access machines is to provide online searching and/or vocationally-oriented educational opportunities, Macintosh or IBM-compatible systems may be more appropriate.

Peripheral devices

Once the computer systems under consideration have been evaluated, the range of peripheral equipment available to expand the capacity of the system will need to be evaluated. Peripherals include devices for input of information, including scanners, digitizers, and bar code readers; for output of information, including printers and projectors; and devices which provide both input and output, including data storage devices and modems for telecommunications activity.

Data storage
The role of data storage in the computer system was touched upon in the section above on evaluating system components. The floppy and hard disk drives mentioned there, however, are far from the only methods available for storing and retrieving information in a microcomputer system. Below, some of the other options are briefly described. The primary issues to consider when choosing data storage media are:

• The amount of information that will need to be stored;

• The types of pre-published information that will need to be retrieved;

• The need for backup and security features; and

• The response time that the medium will provide in accessing to data.

Magnetic media

Although most magnetic storage is accomplished through the use of floppy and hard disk drives, there are several other applications of magnetic technology in data storage. Magnetic tape, for instance, is used in a variety of computer applications. In early microcomputers (most notably the Radio Shack TRS-80), simple cassette tapes and players, identical to those used for recording and playing back audio signals, were used to store and retrieve digital data. Because tape is a linear rather than random access medium, it quickly became impractical for regular use. However, magnetic tape technology has been improved in speed and capacity and is now commonly used for backing up large quantities of information. A range of tape formats are available for data backup activities, and libraries that plan to store large amounts of critical data on hard disk drives should consider purchasing of a tape backup unit for protection of that data.

Magnetic storage is also available in a removable cartridge format through the use of Bernoulli boxes, units which store large quantities of information on a removable cartridge that can be used instead of a hard disk drive. This allows the library to keep critical data in storage when it does not need to be accessed, and also allows for the easy interchange of sets of data.

Optical media

The role of optical storage formats in the microcomputer arena has been growing steadily over the past several years. Optical storage has two important advantages over magnetic storage: first, the data stored on an optical disk is far less vulnerable to loss or damage; and second, the capacity of optical disks is many times that of even the highest-capacity magnetic media.

The most common optical format at present is that of CD-ROM (compact disc read-only memory). CD-ROM discs cannot be used to record data at a workstation, but they provide an ideal format for the distribution of large sets of data, since the capacity of one disc can be as high as 680 MB of information. The rise of database publication in CD-ROM format has had a substantial impact on libraries, since the cost of searching a database can be limited to the fixed cost of the published disc. Thus, libraries can budget fixed amounts for online searching without limiting patron access to databases.

Write-once optical drives (often referred to as WORM drive; write-once read-many) have been available for some time for storing large amounts of data. These drives were used primarily by those who had large amounts of data that needed to be preserved in an archival format. The fact that the drives could not be erased or overwritten limited their usefulness in many environments. Recently, however, erasable optical storage has become available. This technology holds great promise for many applications, although it is still too expensive for most individuals or small organizations.

Printers

The selection of an appropriate printer for a library microcomputer system poses some difficult choices, particularly in public access environments; libraries must take into account both the effect of printer noise upon the library environment, and the need for shared access to these often expensive peripherals. Although acoustical enclosures can decrease printer noise, they cannot silence loud printers completely. Some discussion of printer selection and placement is also contained in Chapter 7, which deals with the design of effective microcomputer work areas.

An excellent source for information on printer technology and extensive reviews of currently available printers is the annual printer review issue of *PC Magazine*, which generally comes out in the fall of each year. Information on ordering back copies of this issue can be obtained by contacting the publisher (see Appendix C).

Some questions to consider when evaluating printers are:

• Is the printer manufactured by a reliable company, and is there a sufficient installed base to ensure adequate technical support?

• Does the printer have both serial and parallel communication capability? If not, can it be expanded to use either?

• Does the printer support multiple print modes (e.g., draft quality and letter quality)? What is the CPS (characters per second) or PPM (pages per minute) rate in each mode?

• Is any programming knowledge necessary to take advantage of special functions?

• How complicated is it to set up the printer (pay particular attention to the need to adjust "dipswitches," which can be difficult to find and use)?

• Is the printer's documentation understandable?

• Will it accommodate both tractor and single sheet stock? Is a sheet feeder available for multiple cut sheets? Can it print mailing labels, envelopes?

• What will the annual cost of replacement ribbons, ink cartridges, or toner be?

• Can the printer be used on a network, or with other printer sharing technologies?

<u>Dot-matrix</u>

Dot-matrix printers are the workhorses of the microcomputer printer world. They are generally the least expensive and most durable, but poorest in terms of print quality of any printer; they are also among the loudest of the printers available for microcomputers, drowned out only by daisy-wheel printers.

The quality of print from dot-matrix printers can vary widely. One of the factors influencing quality is the number of pins used to form each character. The lowest-quality printers are generally 9-pin, and are best used for draft printing, not for correspondence or reports. The highest-quality dot-matrix printers are 24-pin, and some of these printers can produce relatively high-quality text and graphics. Generally, the higher the quality of the output, the slower the speed of the printer. The speed of the printer is rated in terms of number of characters produced per second (CPS). This rate will vary between draft and near-letter-quality (NLQ) modes.

Daisy-wheel

Daisy-wheel printers use an impact print wheel (similar to those used in many electric typewriters) to produce characters, and can be quite loud. The quality of text they produce is quite good, and is comparable to that generated from a standard typewriter. Consider the range of type styles available for the printer, the amount of noise that it makes while operating, the characters per second rate of operation, and the quality of print it produces.

Ink-jet

Recent advances in ink-jet technology have made this type of printer both affordable and quite presentable in its output. Early ink-jet printers suffered from poor print quality, and often required users to print only on expensive, specially treated paper. Today's ink-jet printers will print on standard cut sheet paper (ranging from photocopy to rag bond quality) with a print quality close to that of a laser printer (300 dots per inch).

Ink-jet printing can be an excellent choice for an administrative workstation where low-volume, high-quality printing is necessary. It is less appropriate for a high-volume public access machine, since the ink cartridges are expensive and the print speed is not particularly fast. In addition, users need to beware of getting the printed output wet, since the ink is prone to smudging and smearing.

Laser

Until recently, laser printers were considered a luxury in most microcomputing environments. Their high-quality output was more than balanced by their high prices. As technology for the production of these printers improves, however, the costs are falling. This has made laser printers increasingly affordable peripherals for even tightly budgeted applications.

The primary differentiation among laser printers today is in the area of text and graphics quality. Users whose applications that can utilize the Postscript page description language may wish to consider a Postscript printer. These printers are often twice the cost of non-Postscript printers (at this writing, the lowest-cost Postscript laser printer on the market costs approximately $3,000, after discount), but they provide extremely high-quality graphics and a range of typescript-quality fonts. Postscript printers are common in desktop publishing environments, since they are well-suited to the production of camera-ready text.

Libraries that do not require the range of fonts and graphics that Postscript provides can often find excellent values in the laser printer arena. Since laser printers are often heavily discounted by retailers, it can pay to shop around for the best price.

Things to consider when evaluating laser printers are:

• The availability of Postscript or upgrades to Postscript;

• Compatibility with font cartridges or downloadable fonts;

• The amount of internal memory (which can be used for downloading additional fonts);

• Quality of output (not all 300 dpi printers are created equal); and

• Cost of maintenance and supplies.

Color

Color printers have only recently become available at prices that average users can afford. Until now, only graphic design shops and service bureaus were likely to provide high-quality color output. The range of affordable choices is growing, however, and color printers are legitimate options now even for libraries on tight budgets.

Color is available from some dot-matrix printers, and although the quality is far from perfect, it can be effective for simple graphs and illustrations. A big step up from dot-matrix color, however, is ink-jet color, which can provide very high quality color text and graphics suitable for presentations.

When considering color printers, it is important to evaluate the range of colors that the printer can output, and to ensure that the printer is compatible with the application packages that will be used.

Modems

One of the most common reasons for libraries to invest in microcomputer systems is to take advantage of the many online services now available to the public. Expensive indexes that used to take up valuable shelf space can now be accessed occasionally through online database services; and information that a library might never have been able to offer patrons is now at their fingertips. To access this wealth of online information, however, it is necessary to have the appropriate communications equipment.

The device that computers use to communicate to other computers, whether they be a few blocks away, or across the continent, is a modem. Modems convert information from digital form into analog signals that can be transmitted over ordinary telephone lines, and converts the signals that return over the wire into a digital form that the computer can interpret.

There are several factors that need to be considered when selecting a microcomputer modem. First is the compatibility of the modem with the application software that will be used to establish communication links, and with the software running on the distant (or "host") computer containing the data that will be accessed. The most common standard in microcomputer modem communications is the Hayes standard, which provides the modem with a standard command set for connecting to and communicating with other modems. The purchase of a modem that is Hayes-compatible will ensure that few conflicts will occur in the communications link.

The next issue generally considered in selecting of a modem is the speed at which it will send and receive data, also referred to as the baud rate or bps (bits per second). Although the terms "baud" and "bps" are often used interchangeably to refer to modem speeds, they are not always equivalent; in higher-speed modems, the baud rate can vary significantly from the number of bits per second being transmitted. In this discussion we will use the term bps to represent the modem speed. The minimum rate available on microcomputer modems is 300 bps; the maximum rate is 9600 bps. A 300 bps transfer rate will be very slow and, since many online services charge by the amount of time spent on their system, expensive; 300 bps is therefore not commonly used for online communications. Modems that communicate at 1200 bps are common and inexpensive; 2400 bps modems are becoming increasingly popular. Keep in mind that most higher-speed modems will allow the user to communicate at lower speeds even if the modem on the host computer requires a slower bit rate.

On IBM-compatible microcomputers and Macintosh computers with expansion slots, the issue of internal versus external modems will also need to be considered. Internal modems are contained on expansion cards that need to be placed in one of the computer's internal slots. External modems are connected to the microcomputer through a cable attached to an available serial communications port. On an IBM-compatible, this means one of the 9- or 25-pin serial ports; on a Macintosh the connection is made through a specifically designated modem port that is marked with an icon of a telephone.

Scanners and digitizers

Libraries planning to use their microcomputers for desktop publishing, or to make their computers available to patrons with a strong need for graphics-intensive applications, may wish to consider purchasing of a scanner or digitizer. These peripherals will convert visual images into digital data that can be displayed on a computer screen and modified by graphics programs.

A scanner will take the image from a printed page and convert it into digital data; this digital image can then be read by software on the computer. Two types of software can be used with scanned images: character recognition software will search for images that are in alphanumeric form, and convert them from image to text that can then be manipulated in a text editor or word processor; page recognition software will turn the image into a bit-mapped image that can be modified with graphic arts packages ranging from painting programs to page layout.

A digitizer will allow the conversion of other visual images—for example, the view through the lens of modified camera—into digital format. This can be particularly useful when images from the library surroundings need to be incorporated into documents. One example of this type of applications would be digitizing the images of staff members themselves, and incorporating these computer portraits into newsletters or other library handouts.

Things to consider when evaluating a scanner or digitizer are:

• The number of dots-per-inch (dpi) of its scanned image resolution;

• Speed of operation;

• Capacity to register a range of gray shades; and

• Ease of use.

Projectors

Libraries planning to regularly utilize their microcomputers for training and/or demonstrations should consider the purchase of a projection device. There are a variety of peripherals that allow the user to display the monitor's image onto a projection screen.

One common method for projecting the screen image is to use a projector that intercepts the information being sent from the processor to the monitor, and then uses internal lighting to project that image onto a screen. These units are fairly large and can be difficult to focus effectively.

A newer type of projection device is used in conjunction with an overhead projector. The device itself is a square or rectangular frame around a translucent panel. It can be used in conjunction with, or as a replacement for, the computer's display screen. The image that would be displayed upon the screen is formed on the translucent panel using liquid crystal display technology; the unit is placed on an overhead projector and the image is then projected onto the screen. These devices are less cumbersome to transport, and require less fine-tuning of the display; however, they do require that an overhead projector be available.

Before purchasing any type of projection device, it is important to actually view the image that it is capable of projecting. If possible, this evaluation should be done using the microcomputer that it will most often be used with, to ensure that the unit will be compatible with the library's actual microcomputer configuration. The quality of the image, its visibility from a range of positions within a room, and its ease of use are the primary issues to consider when evaluating these units.

Bar code readers

Libraries that will be using their microcomputers as part of a circulation system should pay close attention to the growing use of bar code technology in library circulation systems. Bar codes (the now omnipresent symbols made up of vertical lines that have appeared on consumer goods ranging from books to bags of candy) are generally associated with cash registers. However, they are also becoming quite common at library check-outs. By issuing library cards with bar codes, patrons can be uniquely identified; likewise, each book in the collection can be tagged with a bar code for quick and easy entering of circulation information into the computer.

All bar code readers, however, are not created equal. Some are more reliable than others, and it is important to talk to users of specific bar code systems before committing to a purchase. Be sure to ask how long the equipment has lasted between failures, about the volume or intrusiveness of the sound emitted by the equipment (and whether the sound can be temporarily or permanently disabled), and about the comfort and ease of use of the light pens or other code scanning devices.

Peripheral sharing

The high cost of many peripherals mentioned above puts a practical limit on the number of these devices a library can purchase. Methods for providing shared access to the equipment often must be implemented. There are two common methods for sharing resources—local area networking and simple switch boxes. A local area network will provide far more features than a basic switch box, but it will do so at a greatly increased cost. Both options are described in more detail in the sections below.

Local area networks

Local area networks (LANs) are becoming increasingly common in all computerized environments, including libraries. The features they offer, including the exchange of files and messages among workstations—even when the computers themselves are made by different manufacturers or utilize different operating systems, the ability to use a central copy of an application program or data file, and the capacity to share peripherals ranging from printers to CD-ROM drives, make them a valuable and useful investment for most automated environments.

There are two factors, however, that can stop a library from installing a LAN. The first factor is funding. The installation of a network generally involves a substantial investment in both hardware and software, as well as the often overlooked cost of the cabling to connect workstations; added to this is the often considerable cost incurred when an outside vendor is hired to configure and/or install the system. The second factor is maintenance; maintaining a LAN requires a much higher degree of technical knowledge than maintaining a stand-alone microcomputer facility. If funding and training issues can be worked out, local area networks can offer excellent resource sharing options to libraries of all types and sizes.

Switch boxes

On a much simpler level, the sharing of peripherals can be accomplished by installing switch boxes that allow several microcomputers to access the same piece of peripheral equipment. Switch boxes are most commonly found in the IBM-PC compatible world, and are most often used to share printers. They can also be used to share any peripheral device that connects to the microcomputer via its serial or parallel communication ports.

Switch boxes can be manual—requiring users to designate, using a mechanical switch, which workstation will have access to a device—or they can be automatic, and will scan the attached computers to determine which workstations are attempting to send information to the peripheral equipment attached. Manual switch boxes are much less expensive, with prices starting from less than fifteen dollars; automatic switches, however, can help prevent misrouting of information, and do not require the users to adjust the box itself. For libraries on a tight budget, a basic switch box can be an excellent method for allowing shared access to limited peripheral equipment.

The primary disadvantage of a switch box for peripheral sharing is its limited range of features. Although it will allow multiple users to share printers, modems, and some other devices, it will not allow the sharing of more complex devices, such as CD-ROM drives. In order to share CD-ROM drives among multiple users, it is necessary to install a full-scale network.

Chapter 6

Cost/Benefit Analysis

One of the primary challenges facing any library when it undertakes a process as potentially complex and far-reaching as the automation of its operations is the question of funding. The decision to automate in a library involves both a substantial commitment of capital funds and a continuing financial responsibility for the upkeep and upgrading of the system, and it is difficult—if not impossible—to justify the expense without a thorough analysis of the costs and benefits of implementing microcomputer technology. Before any commitments can be made, the financial resources available for the purpose of automation must be identified. Linda Bills, in her article entitled "Making Decisions About Automation for Small Libraries," had this to say about automation expenses:

> The cost factor must be considered from two angles—how much will be available to spend and when will these funds be available? Can you afford a fairly large up-front investment with low continuing costs? If so, a locally owned system—either single user or shared—is indicated. Or can you better arrange to make regular payments over a long period of time? When you are calculating the size of the investment, don't plan to get a system that will cost most of the amount you have available; automation always costs more than you expect. Either there are extra preparations you must

make so it will be most effective, or you find that it will work even better with some additional component.[3]

This chapter addresses in more detail the issues that Ms. Bills raises. It will assist library automation planners in determining both the costs and the benefits of an automated system, ranging from the expense of the actual equipment to the value of increased productivity the use of automated tools can bring.

Expenses

It is rare for the cost of an automation project to meet or fall below the original expectations of the planners: there are a variety of hidden costs in the purchase of microcomputer equipment. It is particularly important not to use information from published advertisements as the basis for price projections, as these ads can provide misleading information regarding overall system cost. More often than not, advertised prices do not include such items as display monitor and disk drives. In addition, these advertisements do not necessarily reflect discounts available for institutional or volume purchases. It is, therefore, essential that managers assemble the information about required system components and approach vendors for complete price quotations. The information provided in the following section should help managers identify the full range of expenses that can be anticipated.

Equipment costs

The most obvious expense associated with automation is the cost of the equipment itself. But even this expense can easily be misrepresented by vendors trying to make prices look more reasonable. The cost of a microcomputer is often much higher than the price that one sees advertised. For instance, a price shown in an ad for a computer system

---

[3]Bills, Linda G. "Making decisions about automation for small libraries." *Library Resources & Technical Services*, v. 29, Apr./June 1985: 161-171.

may show a remarkably low price—but that price is unlikely to include such "options" as a monitor and a keyboard. When soliciting prices from vendors, a list of required components should always be provided to the vendor, and a list of components included in the vendor's offering should always be received with any quote or bid. It is important to understand the many parts that make up a computer system, so that all the costs can be evaluated.

The cost of the system begins with the cost of the microcomputer unit itself. The components of the equipment that need to be considered are not only the main system unit (also known as the CPU), but also the floppy disk drives and hard drives, internal memory (RAM), the monitor, expansion cards (including graphics adapters), and available ports for communication to other devices (some types of ports are serial ports, parallel ports, and SCSI ports). All of these components were discussed in detail in the system features section of Chapter 5. Short definitions of many of these terms can be found in the glossary contained in Appendix A.

In addition to the system unit, there is the expense of peripheral equipment, used for input and output of information. As described in Chapter 5, this includes a range of devices from printers and plotters to scanners and bar code readers. During the needs assessment process, basic requirements for input and output of information should have been defined; these requirements can then be used to identify the specific peripheral devices that will be required for use in the initial system configuration.

Another issue to consider in hardware pricing is the current status of the model being sold in the manufacturer's product line. Quite often, a price that looks too good to be true is an indication that the vendor is attempting to "unload" hardware that is no longer manufactured and may soon not be maintainable. Beware of close-out sales; a short-term savings of a few hundred dollars may be erased by the expense of replacing components that can no longer be repaired a year later.

Libraries on a tight budget may wish to consider leasing hardware from a vendor. A growing number of computer retailers are offering lease options on their microcomputer equipment, and for libraries that cannot afford the initial capital outlay for purchasing the equipment, but expect to have a regular source of funding for the equipment over a period of time, this can be an excellent solution.

Software costs

Like hardware costs, software costs are not always as easy to calculate as they might appear. With many IBM-compatible microcomputers, the operating system is not included in the purchase of the system, and must be purchased separately; this is the first software cost to be considered, since without an operating system, application software cannot be run.

Once the computer type and operating system have been determined, the list of required applications generated during the needs assessment process can be used to identify specific application programs that can be run on the system of choice.

When selecting software, it is crucial that research be done on the available programs in every application area. Comparative reviews are often the most useful when the first software is being chosen for use on a system, and there are a number of excellent sources for good comparative reviews: system specific journals, such as those listed in Appendix C, are often the best place to start; most of these journals are indexed in Microcomputer Index, which is available in print, online, and CD-ROM formats. Another excellent source for comparative reviews of software products is the *Datapro Reports on Microcomputers*; this is a looseleaf publication updated regularly to keep pace with the rapid changes in microcomputer software. These reports are expensive, but can often be found in large academic or public libraries.

Many libraries will find that the same pressures which led them to choose a given hardware configuration—patron needs, organizational standards, or purchasing restrictions—will also guide their choice of application software. When this happens, the emphasis will need to be on finding the best available prices, as opposed to the most cost-effective program. The process of evaluating vendors, for both hardware and software purchases, is discussed later in this chapter.

Once a software application has been selected, the number of copies of that package that will be needed should be determined. Software licensing agreements for most commercial programs prohibit the use of a single copy of the program on multiple microcomputers; in order to avoid violating copyright law, sufficient licensed copies of the application for all computers that will be running it must be purchased. If the organization will be using a large number of copies of a specific package, the option of site licenses should be explored. A site license is a special license granted by a software publisher that allows an organization to distribute a program for use on all of its microcomputers in exchange for a single set fee that is paid to the publisher. These licenses can save a great deal of money when the number of units required is high. In large companies or institutions, a site license may already exist for those applications being used widely; the computer center or computer support staff should be contacted before software is purchased to determine whether site licenses are available for any programs being considered for purchase.

Libraries with the freedom to select applications without adhering to predefined standards—particularly those with a small budget for software—should be sure to consider the many application programs available as public domain software (which can be distributed to all users with no copyright or royalty payments required) and/or "shareware" (which can be distributed freely, but requires users of the program to send a small contribution to the program's author to support his or her development efforts). Current versions of many shareware and public domain programs are available from users groups and bulletin board services, as well.

Furniture and accessories costs

Included in the initial budget for a new microcomputer system should be the furniture needed to house it, and the consumable accessories that accompany it. There are a variety of specially designed tables and desks designed for ergonomic use of microcomputer equipment. If the budget can support purchase of such furniture, it can be ideal for library use. If the budget will not allow for this purchase, however, it is possible to use existing tables and desks for the computer equipment, although the resulting work areas may not be as comfortable for users to work at.

Another furniture item that should be considered is a printer stand for each printer being purchased. The stand will serve multiple functions. First, it will provide a steady base for a piece of equipment that requires a solid place to sit. Second, it often will provide shelves upon which printer paper and supplies can be placed, resulting in a more convenient configuration.

Although they are often forgotten in the budgeting process, the expense of printer supplies, diskettes, and cleaning supplies should be included in the initial budget. If the printer is a dot-matrix or daisy-wheel that uses continuous sheet perforated paper, boxes of pin-feed paper should be purchased for the initial setup. There are many varieties of pin-feed paper, ranging from the lowest-quality rag content and roughest perforations to high-rag content paper with "invisible" perforations. The type of paper purchased should reflect the type of printing that will be done most often on the printer; draft quality prints do not need high quality paper, whereas correspondence and reports may not be appropriately printed on low-quality paper. Dot-matrix and daisy-wheel printers will also require ribbons, and these should be ordered in advance, as well.

If the printer is a laser or ink-jet printer, it will probably use single sheet paper (dot-matrix and daisy-wheel printers with sheet feeders will also be able to use single sheet paper). This widens the choice of paper available; anything that can be used in a photocopier or typewriter can probably be used in the printer (the printer manual should be checked to verify any possible paper incompatibilities).

Laser printers will generally require toner cartridges rather than ribbons, and ink-jet printers use ink cartridges. Like printer ribbons, these can often be purchased through office supply stores as well as through computer dealers. Be sure to check around to find the best price.

The new computer facility will also need a stock of blank diskettes. It is important to determine exactly what type of diskette the system being ordered will require, since many diskettes can be used only in a single type of disk drive. It is not sufficient to know that the disks should be 5-1/4" or 3-1/2" inches. It is also necessary to know whether the disks should be single or double-sided, and whether they should be low or high density.

Although high-density drives can read and write to low-density disks, low-density drives *cannot* read or write to high-density disks; when in doubt, choosing a low-density diskette is therefore less risky.

Environmental preparation costs

If this is the first investment a library is making in microcomputer equipment, there will probably be a number of expenses related to preparation of the physical environment to support the computers. In Chapter 7 these environmental issues are described in more detail; they should, however, also be considered in this process of determining total system cost.

The two most important, and potentially expensive, environmental factors to consider are electrical power supply and air quality. Without a reliable source of electric current, computer equipment will not function properly, and will be prone to regular (and expensive) breakdowns. Without a clean air supply with a regulated level of humidity, similar problems will occur. If the setting in which the computers will be placed does not have modern electrical wiring (with three-hole grounded outlets), and air conditioning, the expense of installing these features should be included in the initial cost of the system.

Even in a building with a reliable power supply, it is advisable to include the relatively small cost of surge protectors for each computer in the initial budget. A surge suppressor is a multiple outlet power strip that will screen some fluctuations in electrical current before they can do damage to the microcomputer's internal components. They generally cost less than $30.00, and can save substantial repair expenses in the future. More information on surge suppressors can be found in Chapter 11, which deals with preventive maintenance issues.

Staffing costs

If the microcomputer facility being proposed is a large-scale one, and if it will be used for public access computing, the potential need for additional full or part-time staff members should be considered. A public access computing facility needs to be closely monitored for two primary reasons: first, to provide patrons with assistance in using the equipment, and second, to prevent the theft and/or abuse of the equipment and software.

In a large library it may be possible to reallocate staff resources to provide consistent coverage of the microcomputer facility. In a smaller library, however, it may be necessary to hire new staff members to provide this service. This need should be factored into the cost of the microcomputer project, since it can add substantially to the start-up and ongoing cost of the system.

Training costs

Regardless of the size or scope of the proposed facility, training costs for staff members must be included in the initial budget for the project. Without sufficient training for the users of the system, the computers will be used ineffectively, if at all. Training can be done outside of the library, by sending selected staff members to a training facility in the area, or it can be done in the library, by bringing in an instructor or by providing self-paced training materials. Whichever option is chosen, it should be considered a mandatory item in the budgeting of both time and funds. More information on the training and orientation process is contained in Chapter 8.

Maintenance costs

It is all too easy for planners to forget that computer equipment is never failure-proof. The long-term costs of maintenance and upgrading of the computer system must be included in the cost/benefit analysis. There are a variety of ways that maintenance costs can be handled, and these options are discussed in Chapter 13 of this book.

Return on investment

The list of costs associated with a new computer system can be daunting; but as we discussed in Chapter 3, most libraries that have made this investment have found that the benefits far outweighed the costs. In the February 15, 1983 issue of *Library Journal*, Robert M. Mason addressed the concerns of many librarians regarding the justification for purchasing expensive microcomputer equipment:

> The decision to buy a micro had been made with caution, and the process of deciding which one had consumed several months. I had hesitated, considering all the factors that everyone seems to mention when they explain their reasons for waiting: "The technology is changing rapidly." "I don't know if I can justify it on the basis of cost." . . . My decision was bold, I thought: I will buy one because I believe that I can get my investment back (through improved productivity of the research and consulting efforts) within two years.
>
> Within six months (after finally getting the system operating), I realized how mistaken I had been. I was convinced that the computer already had paid for itself, and I was arranging for the purchase of two others.[4]

Many of the benefits of library automation were discussed in Chapter 3, in the needs assessment process. The primary issues are described again in this chapter, for the purpose of integrating this information into the cost justification for the microcomputer facility.

Increased productivity

When microcomputers are used to automate either the management and clerical functions of the library, or the library-specific areas of operation, the jump in productivity can be astounding. This productivity can reduce costs in many ways. First, it can eliminate some of the needs for non-professional support staff, as well as many needs for outside services.

One good example in the management and clerical area is the use of art and/or page-layout programs to produce brochures, handouts, and

---

[4]Mason, Robert M. "Choosing a microcomputer: a success story." *Library Journal*, v. 108, Feb. 15, 1983: 356-358.

signs for the library. Many items which needed to be painstakingly cut and pasted from paper, or were sent out to graphic arts service bureaus, can be produced with ease on a microcomputer system. (One caveat, however—the possession of a page layout program does not necessarily make one a page layout artist. Those libraries choosing to produce their own graphic designs should invest not only in training on the computer system, but also in training in basic design concepts.)

In the library automation area, the automation of the circulation system can help eliminate such tedious tasks of culling files by hand for overdue books and preparing letters for patrons with overdue materials; it also can streamline the process of placing holds for material that is checked out.

The list of tasks that should be automated which was prepared in the needs assessment process will be the best tool for preparing an analysis of possible cost-savings that would result from the installation of microcomputer tools.

Improved access to information resources

Another important factor in justifying the investment in microcomputer technology is the range of information sources that can only be accessed by libraries with the appropriate automated tools. As we discussed in Chapter 5, the proliferation of information resources in machine-readable form—ranging from CD-ROM databases to the wealth of online information resources available on such services as DIALOG and BRS—makes a microcomputer a necessity for a library that wishes to provide its patrons with a full range of reference sources. A single investment in a microcomputer with a modem will enable a library to access a wealth of information in electronic form; information that would otherwise need to be purchased in print form, which takes up valuable shelf space and financial resources.

The argument of expanded access to electronic information resources is a strong one in the justification of a microcomputer system in a library. It can be backed up with surveys of patron needs, and cost comparisons between occasional searches of an online resource and purchase of the printed version of that resource.

Expanded services for patrons

When the microcomputer facility being planned is intended for public access use, the justification for the expense is clear. Not only can microcomputers provide patrons with access to the information resources described above, they also provide patrons with the opportunity to overcome "computer illiteracy." As computers become an increasingly important part of our educational and business environments, those individuals without training and experience in computers are put at a disadvantage. Just as libraries provide resources to assist patrons in overcoming traditional illiteracy, so they have a responsibility to provide their patrons with tools to "read" information in this new electronic age. This is a powerful argument in the justification of a public access microcomputing facility.

Chapter 7

Purchase and Installation

Once the plans have been written, the systems have been evaluated, and the budget has been approved, the purchase and installation of the microcomputer system can finally begin. This chapter addresses the issues involved with these two steps in the microcomputer management process.

The first part of the chapter deals with the selection of a vendor (or vendors) for the purchase of the hardware and software components of the system. The chapter then continues with a discussion of the issues involved with preparing a physical environment for the computers. Finally, a step-by-step approach for receiving, unpacking, and installing the new equipment is provided.

Selection of vendors

The proliferation of computer hardware and software vendors has made it difficult for anyone purchasing a new computer system to know where to turn for good prices, expert assistance, and high-quality support. Although it can be difficult to tell a reliable vendor from a fly-by-night store front at first glance, there are a number of verifiable factors that can be identified as part of a good dealership. Some libraries may be bound to an institutional purchasing contract that dictates their choice of vendors;

those which have to start from scratch, however, will be best served by evaluating a range of vendors. A minimum of three vendors should always be evaluated when a new purchase agreement is being considered.

The most obvious point of comparison among vendors is the price that they charge for their hardware, but the cost of the individual components of a system should be only one factor in the decision of which vendor to use. Purchasing a system at rock-bottom prices from the cheapest mail-order house around may save some money up front, but most buyers end up paying for these short term savings in frustration and ongoing maintenance problems. This is not to say that the dealer with the lowest prices—sometimes even mail-order vendors—cannot be the best choice for purchasing. It is only to say that before making a substantial capital investment in a computer system, any buyer would be well advised to carefully evaluate the vendors under consideration, using the criteria described below.

References

The first place to start in compiling a short list of viable alternatives is with references from satisfied users. Some of these references probably emerged during the planning process, during visits to other libraries. Other sources for such information are local users groups, and the vendor itself—if the vendor *cannot* provide a list of references to satisfied customers, that alone is reason enough to view the business with suspicion. Questions about all of the issues below that are of importance to the library should be asked of the references; if possible, the references contacted should be those with configuration similar to that being considered for purchase, and those using their computers for similar applications.

Financial stability

Even if a vendor's references are good, it is important to do some research on the stability of the company. The computer business is very volatile, and there is a high rate of failure among computer dealers. Some things to inquire about are: How long has the company been in business? Is it owned by a larger company? What are the total sales figures and projections for past and current year? How many staff members are employed, at all locations and at the location that will be the primary point of contact? And is the vendor an "authorized" dealer for the product line being considered? (Vendors without the official seal of approval are probably lacking in technical support for some products, since they are unlikely to be able to contact the manufacturer as easily as an authorized dealer.)

Support and training

One of the strongest reasons for purchasing a computer system from a local business is the support that the vendor can provide. However, the fact that a vendor is located nearby does not always guarantee that they can provide high-quality support.

There are two areas in which technical support can be crucial. The first is in configuring the initial system. A well-trained salesperson will be able to assist purchasers in selecting components that will best meet their stated needs, and will not attempt to sell unnecessary hardware or software to the customer. The second important area for support is that of assistance during the setup and initial use of the system, when the greatest number of problems are likely to arise. A good vendor will be able to provide technical support over the telephone to the staff members responsible for setting up the new microcomputer systems.

Closely related to the technical support issue is that of training. A vendor that has made a commitment to providing structured training courses or materials for its customers is also likely to be able to provide trained support on an ongoing basis. Even if the library chooses to arrange its training through another source, the existence of a training program is a positive sign in the evaluation of a systems vendor.

Warranties and service

Although a new microcomputer may look like it will last forever, computer equipment of all kinds is notoriously fallible. It is important, therefore, to determine the warranty coverage for any items being purchased, and the service options that will be available from the dealer both during and after the warranty period. Many of these maintenance issues are discussed in more detail in the maintenance sections of this book, but should be touched upon in the initial evaluation of a vendor. There are a number of questions that should be asked of any vendor regarding its ability to provide service. Will repair work be done in-house? Can loaners be provided while equipment is being repaired? Is on-site service available? What is the technician-to-customer ratio? Does the vendor provide telephone support? What is the per hour charge for maintenance after the warranty period ends?

Mail-order vendors

Mail-order vendors present a difficult choice for computer purchasers. On the one hand, mail-order houses can usually provide by far the best prices for both hardware and software. On the other hand, when dealing with a long-distance supplier, even the smallest frustrations with service and support can be magnified by the problems in communication. (It is a lot harder to ignore an angry customer at your counter than it is to put an angry telephone caller on hold.)

Recently, a number of mail-order vendors have improved the quality of their technical support in several ways. First, these vendors provide a high-quality telephone support line, staffed by technicians who can walk puzzled users through all the preliminary trouble-shooting steps over the telephone. Second, several of these vendors have also teamed up with national companies like Whirlpool to provide on-site service to all the computers they sell. With these enhancements, mail-order computers can indeed provide not only excellent price, but also excellent value.

However, it is not always easy to tell which mail-order vendors are likely to provide customers with reliable, high-performance components. *PC Magazine* does occasionally review the state of the mail-order business, and includes major mail-order offerings in its reviews of computer systems. Users groups and electronic bulletin boards can often yield recommendations or warnings regarding well-known mail-order companies.

Preparation for installation

Once a system has been settled on, a vendor selected, and system purchased, preparations need to be made for the arrival of the new equipment. These preparations include the design of appropriate working areas, the purchase or modification of furniture, any modifications that will need to be made to electrical power or air supply, and consideration of security needs for hardware and software.

Design of effective work areas

When microcomputer workstations are being installed for the first time, it is important for planners to realize that the requirements for an ergonomically correct computer workstation are not the same as those for a traditional work area. The lighting requirements, desk height requirements, and even the type of chair recommended may vary substantially from those used in the past.

The issues relating to layout of a computer facility are many and varied, and will not be covered here in detail. There are a number of books and articles dealing with these concerns, and several are listed in the bibliography in Appendix B. One particularly useful book is *Developing Microcomputer Work Areas in Academic Libraries*, edited by Jeannine Uppgard.[5] Although the book is made up of descriptions of academic library computing facilities, many of the issues and solutions described by the contributors are common to all library settings.

Furniture and storage equipment

Before computer equipment can be installed, it is important to have adequate furniture to house the components and the various accessories that accompany them. The place to begin is with the desks or tables upon which the system units will sit. To be ergonomically correct, the computers should sit so that the monitors are approximately at eye level,

---

[5]*Developing microcomputer work areas in academic libraries*. Westport, CT, Meckler, 1988. 124 p.

and the keyboards are not higher than a users' elbows. It is not always possible to order tables that are designed with these requirements in mind; however, it is often possible to modify existing furniture by adding such items as slide-out keyboard drawers, or by placing system units on their sides next to the desk, rather than upon it.

Also important to consider are the needs for placing printers. If the printer is noisy (dot-matrix or daisy-wheel) and will be placed in a public area, some sort of acoustic noise-reducing cover should be considered. Without some sort of hood or box over the printer, the noise it emits can be distracting to all library patrons.

Once the equipment has been provided for, some other issues need to be considered, particularly in the areas of storage and access. Where will software programs be stored? Where will manuals be kept? Where will diskettes and printer supplies be located? Appropriate cabinets and bookshelves will have to be purchased for these items. If possible, metal furniture should be avoided for storage of diskettes and software, since the risks of static discharge and magnetic charge are increased. A balance must be struck between ease of access and security concerns; the issue of security is discussed in more detail later in this chapter.

Environmental requirements

The issues involved with the microcomputer working environment were discussed in Chapter 6 under "Expenses," and are also discussed in Chapter 11, under "Preventive maintenance." An inspection of the physical surroundings and a quick check to be sure that all requirements are met should be done during the pre-installation process, too.

There are several items to check for during this inspection. The first is the number of electrical outlets available near workstations. Many computer configurations require at least two grounded outlets; if a printer or other peripherals will be nearby, the number of outlets needed will increase, and a power strip of some kind will be required. Even if there are sufficient outlets, the purchase of a power strip with surge protection capabilities is a prudent purchase, since it will protect the equipment from power surges and spikes while providing additional outlets for expansion.

If any of the computers will be used for telecommunication, the area should also be checked to ensure that a telephone outlet is available. If the library is on a private phone system, or PBX, as are many large companies and institutions, it may be necessary to consult with the telephone system vendor to find out if any special equipment is necessary to use the telephone line for data communications.

It is important to have adequate lighting in the work areas. If overhead lighting is not available, desk lamps should be placed liberally around the work area, taking care not to create glare on the monitor screens. Lighting for computer use should be indirect, rather than direct, and should not be too harsh.

Security concerns

Computer systems and software are expensive items, and as such, are always tempting targets for theft. In addition, the growing phenomenon of malicious and often destructive programs called viruses or worms present a new threat to library computers that must be guarded against. Libraries need to take measures to secure their systems, particularly in public access computing facilities.

On the physical front, there are a number of ways to protect against theft of computer components. A number of manufacturers provide kits which allow the cabling of the key system components to the desk or table it sits on. This is particularly common in the Macintosh accessory market. It is also possible to mark components with some sort of "brand," using a carving tool or indelible marker on the case of the equipment. Although this will not prevent theft, it will serve as a deterrent, and will allow for easier recovery of stolen goods. (Records of the serial numbers of all equipment should also be kept, and will be valuable information for equipment inventories, as well as for identifying recovered equipment.)

Installing the equipment

Now that the planning is done, the preparations are complete, and the boxes are sitting on the floor of the library, the process of actually installing the new systems can begin. In most cases, this is not a terribly difficult task; however, for those new to computers, it can be time-consuming. The information below covers the installation process in a step-by-step manner; for detailed information on installing a specific system, however, it will be necessary to consult the documentation that will be shipped with the system.

Verifying inventory

The first step in installing a recently purchased system is always to ensure that the packing lists from the boxes match the order that was placed to the vendor, *and* that the contents of the boxes match the packing lists. It is all too common for errors to be made in the shipping process, and it is much easier to correct them before extensive setting up and customization has been done. If portions of the order are missing, or have been filled with equipment that does not match the specifications, the dealer should be contacted immediately for instructions on how to obtain the proper components.

All of the packing lists should be saved, and kept with the original copies of the order; they will need to be checked against the invoices when they arrive, if the equipment was not paid for in advance. They also provide a valuable record of equipment received, and will form the basis for an ongoing inventory list.

Unpacking equipment

Once the boxes have been determined to hold the appropriate equipment, the task of removing the components from the ingenious packaging in which it is housed begins. Several tools will be useful in this activity: a sharp knife, carton opener, razor blade, or scissors for opening the carton itself and any plastic bags inside; a box into which small parts can be placed so as not to lose them in the mess; and a file folder in which all documentation, including manuals and registration cards, can be kept temporarily.

The boxes themselves, and any molded styrofoam pieces inside that hold the equipment in place, should *not* be thrown away. If for any reason the system needs to be returned or repaired, the safest method for shipping it to a dealer or repair facility is in its original packaging. Put these materials into a safe storage area.

The registration materials, although they may instruct the buyer to fill them out immediately, should be put aside until the components have been tested and found to perform satisfactorily.

Setting up and testing components

When the system has been unpacked, it should be assembled (if necessary) and set up according to the documentation accompanying it. The procedure will vary considerably based upon the brand and configuration of the system purchased.

Once the hardware has been properly set up, it should be connected to a power source and turned on. All power indicators on the computer should turn on properly; if they do not, the dealer should be contacted immediately.

In order to test the hardware components, it is necessary to start the computer using the operating system. On computers with hard drives, the dealer will often have installed the operating system onto the drive already. If this is not the case, the documentation will usually provide clear directions for installation. On computers without hard drives, the operating system will be run from the floppy disk each time the computer is turned on.

Installing software

After hardware has been shown to be operational, the software can be installed. On a system with a hard drive, the operating system should be loaded onto the hard drive first, and the application software should be installed according to the directions contained in the documentation. On a system using only floppy disks, the software will be run directly from its original diskettes, and less installation will be involved.

During the process of software installation, some incompatibilities may surface. On an IBM-compatible system, certain system files (specifically, the CONFIG.SYS and AUTOEXEC.BAT files) may need to be created or reconfigured properly in order for application programs to run. On a Macintosh system, since there are fewer user-configurable options in the system software, there are fewer potential incompatibilities when software is first installed; however, if the computer was configured with insufficient memory for the application, some problems may appear. In either case, the vendor of the software should be able to assist in pinpointing specific causes for problems, and in offering solutions for those problems.

Registration cards

Once the system has been shown to work properly, it is essential that the registration cards shipped with both the hardware and the software be filled out and mailed immediately. Properly registering the items has two primary benefits. First, it allows the owner to take advantage of any technical support or warranty programs offered by the manufacturer. Second, it ensures that the owner will receive any information from the manufacturer regarding updates, changes, or additions to the program or equipment.

When the cards have been completed, they should be photocopied, and the copy should be filed along with the purchasing information for the item; it may be useful if problems arise with the item at a later date.

Chapter 8

Orientation and Training

No matter how much time is spent planning for, evaluating, purchasing, and installing microcomputer equipment in order to maximize its usefulness, the time will be wasted if an effort is not also made to prepare the staff for the changes in their work routines that will result from the new automation. Unless the staff is convinced to 'buy into' the process of automation, and their support is secured for the microcomputer facility, the computers will at best be resented and underutilized. At worst, they could well result in the alienation and even resignation of key members of the staff.

Professor Paul Ansfield, a member of the Psychology Department of the University of Wisconsin in Oshkosh, wrote in *Catholic Library World*:

> When any new device or procedure is installed, an abrupt change in how we behave or do our work is called for. With the installation of the heralded, and largely unfamiliar microcomputer, abrupt changes are certain and may be severe. At the outset, the naive employee does not understand what the installation of a microcomputer really portends. Therein lies the threat, physical discomfort of stress, and the strong

feelings which arise when the machine arrives with little warning or planning.[6]

There are many ways a manager can lessen the negative impact of microcomputer installation upon his or her staff. Before you begin preparing them for the changes ahead, however, it is important to understand what factors are influencing their reactions, and what issues you will be able to address most effectively in order to improve their response to the new computers. This chapter addresses both the causes of employee resistance to new methods of operation, and some methods for reducing this resistance through appropriate orientation and training both before and after the machines arrive.

Resistance to change

Resistance to change in an organization is not a new phenomenon, and is not limited to the areas of technological change. However, the rate of change in technological fields has resulted in an increased prominence of this reluctance to adopt new working conditions and activities. As was discussed in the chapters on planning, it is extremely important to involve employees in the planning process; this allows them to develop a feeling of personal investment in the success of the new automated system. Employees *must* feel as though their needs are being considered and addressed as decisions are made about microcomputer equipment and installation.

Fear of new technology often asserts itself as overt hostility. Emphasizing the limitations of the new computers along with their abilities, may help dispel fears that the computers will take over library operations or displace current workers.

These reactions to the change associated with new automated systems are not limited to the library environment. In fact, libraries have

---

[6]Ansfield, Paul J. "Humanizing the installation of microcomputers." *Catholic Library World*, v. 54, Nov. 1982: 151-154.

the advantage of learning from the experiences of businesses that have already gone through the process of integrating new technology into the workplace. Below are excerpts from a list of "installation tips" that appeared in a management magazine in 1983, as part of an article addressing the installation of office computers:[7]

- Don't expect immediate change. Begin installation on a gradual, fairly small basis.

- New technology must be integrated with existing systems. From an economic as well as an acceptance standpoint, this is more desirable than wholesale replacement of equipment.

- Heavily involve the potential users of the new equipment in the decision-making process. Not only will this soothe feelings, but it will also result in practical suggestions which will save money in the long run.

- Before any system can be productive, the users must receive effective, continuous training. Programs for training must be intense, non-threatening and encourage immediate use.

- Follow-up training should be made available when needed.

- No one should be forced to use new equipment if they are adamantly against it. Resentment often leads to sabotage in one form or another. Those who are most resistant will eventually come around when they see that those who are adapting fastest are being rewarded for increased productivity.

- Realistically, some companies may have to wait for computer literacy to spread throughout their organization, possibly through retirement and attrition.

Pre-installation orientation

If the library has a small staff, chances are that most, if not all, have been involved in the planning process before the machines actually arrive. If this is the case, the initial stress that accompanies abrupt change

---

[7]Seaward, Marty Robertson. "Awakening to office automation." *MW*, May 1983: 27-30.

will be greatly reduced. Staff members who have had little or no involvement in the process of evaluating and selecting the equipment to be used will have the greatest difficulty adjusting to the changes in their work routines. It is important for *all* employees to be involved in orientation programs before the equipment arrives. These sessions are critical to giving staff the information they need in order to adapt to the changes ahead. They also play a role in helping staff members feel as though they have some degree of control over the process of change.

If scheduled orientation programs are not possible given staff scheduling constraints, information on the upcoming changes and how they will affect the staff should be distributed in written form, with plenty of time allowed for concerns to be raised and questions to be asked and answered.

Some items to consider presenting to staff in this pre-installation period are: a description of the system to be installed, and what functions it will perform; an explanation of which jobs will be affected by the installation of the system, and how; a schedule for installation *and* for staff training; and a bibliography of books and articles that staff can use to expand their own understanding of the role of automated systems in the library, as well as to better understand the specific system being installed.

This type of preparation is invaluable; it should not, however, be used in place of training for all users of the system. It is designed to prepare people for the changes on a far more general level, and must still be supplemented with training activities that will provide staff members with the specific skills they will need to use when the tools are in place.

In-house vs. outside training

There are two options available to libraries for training staff to use microcomputer equipment and applications. The first is to do the training in-house, using library staff members, or other experienced computer users in the organization—from the systems or data processing office, for example. The second option is to use an outside training facility, and send some or all staff members to training classes with professional instructors.

Each of these options has both advantages and disadvantages associated with it.

In-house training

In order to do in-house training effectively, a library must be able to provide two primary resources. The first requirement is that staff members with knowledge of the computer system and software, as well as experience in development and presentation of training materials, must be available to conduct the classes. This is not a requirement that can be glossed over; a training class presented by an instructor who has inadequate knowledge of the subject matter *or* poor presentation skills will not provide staff members with the information that they require.

The second requirement is the availability of an area in the library that can be set up as a training classroom, complete with working computers. To be effective, a training class on microcomputer use *must* allow the students to have "hands-on" opportunities during the class. If the computers are not available, it will be very difficult for the students to associate the concepts being presented with the actual activities to which they must be applied.

If these two requirements can be met, in-house training can be a very cost-effective method for training staff members in the use of a new system. Offering the training on-site means that staff members spend a minimum amount of time away from their jobs. It also allows the customization of a training program, not just to a given site, but to the specific groups of employees who will be attending the class.

Even if full training activities cannot be offered on-site, the project manager for the microcomputer installation should prepare some documentation that will be specific to the library staff's needs. The documentation should be easily accessible near the terminals that staff will use. One useful format is that of a "quick reference card"; another possibility is to put key information on the system in poster format and hang it near each computer.

Outside training

Libraries that do not have the resources to offer training classes in-house generally have a variety of outside training sources available to them. The computer training business is booming, and end users can benefit from this proliferation of services. Training facilities can be affiliated with a computer hardware or software vendor—for example, The Computer Factory and Egghead Software, both national chains, offer a range of software training classes—or can be independently operated businesses. Other centers can be identified through the yellow pages, advertisements in local newspapers, users groups, electronic bulletin boards, and references from other users.

If the system being installed at the library is a special-purpose system designed primarily for library-specific automation, it is likely that the vendor of the equipment and/or software will be the best source of information on appropriate training courses. In any case, users of similar systems—who should have been identified early in the planning process, as well as in the process of obtaining references for vendors—can also provide suggestions for outside training options.

Once training facilities have been identified—through advertisements, directory listings, or recommendations by users or vendors—they should be evaluated by the planning team. The first step in evaluation is to examine the schedules of training classes. If the courses that the library staff will require are not being offered regularly, or if the range of courses being offered is limited, this may be a drawback; even if the facility is willing to offer the classes required on a one-time basis, there would be no way to assess the quality of such a class in advance, or to guarantee with any degree of certainty that the class would be available on an ongoing basis if additional training needs arose.

Once the available choices for training have been narrowed down based on recommendations and review of curricula, the next step is to evaluate the facilities in more detail. There are several components to this type of evaluation.

The first step is to interview representatives from the training facility, paying specific attention to the areas they emphasize in their training; do they work toward making students self-sufficient, or are they more interested in fostering a dependent relationship with the training center? Do they provide students with useful materials for post-class work? Is there any sort of guarantee provided for refunds or second offerings of a class when a student feels the material has not been adequately covered? The specific materials and outline used in the classes should be obtained for review purposes.

The next step is to have a staff member—preferably one that already has some familiarity with the subject matter—sit in on a class to evaluate its content and presentation. Most training centers will allow this type of evaluation at no charge. It is important to try to schedule courses with similar content at each facility, so as to provide a consistent basis for comparison.

Finally, the issue of pricing needs to be considered. If the library will be sending more than two or three staff members for training, it is likely that some sort of group discount can be negotiated. If a long-term agreement for provision of training services can be signed, often the cost savings can be substantial.

The high competition in the computer training arena today has resulted in a marked improvement in the quality of instruction. Using an outside trainer for library automation projects can be an excellent way to effectively train staff members over a period of time, and will allow for the maintenance of a consistent standard of training.

Combining training methods

There are several options for training that combine elements of both in-house and outside training methods. Many libraries will find that using one of these "compromise" methods will allow them to customize a training program with maximum effectiveness as well as minimum cost.

Recently, a number of training centers have begun to offer on-site training options. They will provide the course materials, instructor, and in some cases even the computers; the client provides the space and the students. This allows the convenience of on-site training and customization of a class, without the investment in a full-time trainer or internal training center.

Another option utilizing both inside and outside training is to designate several staff members as key trainers within the library, and to send these people for training in all aspects of the system. If possible, it can also be helpful to send these individuals to classes on the best methods for training others on computer related topics—these "training the trainer" courses are offered by a number of training centers. Once these individuals have been trained, they can then train other staff members in small groups. Ideally, these internal training sessions can even be held in the work areas of the employees being trained, and will be specifically tailored to their individual needs.

These are only two of the possibilities that can emerge through the combination of internal and external training resources; each library will need to assess its own needs and resources to determine what method of training will best suit its environment. One factor in this decision will be the type of activities for which training will be needed; the sections below outline the training needs that are likely to be associated with the various types of library automation.

Training for administrative operations

Libraries automating their administrative functions are likely to have the least trouble in locating appropriate training facilities or internal trainers. The use of standardized software packages—those used in a wide range of offices and institutions—expands the range of choices substantially. The many training centers catering to business needs will also be able to provide appropriate training to staff members needing instruction in word processing, database management, spreadsheet use, and telecommunications, as well as networking and integration activities.

There is little need to consider these training needs in a library-specific light, since they mirror the needs of any organization undergoing a change to an automated environment; the information provided in the sections above should be sufficient for the identification and implementation of appropriate training methods.

Training for library-specific operations

When a library puts into place a system designed to automate such library-specific operations as circulation, cataloging, or acquisitions, the training needs become more complex. It is unrealistic to expect that commercial training facilities will be equipped to meet the library's more specialized requirements; in fact, in most cases they will probably be completely unfamiliar with the software being implemented. (The exception to this would be smaller libraries in which library-developed "templates" for commercial applications are being utilized.)

Often, the only viable option for outside training is to arrange for classes to be conducted by the system vendor or its designated representative. These classes may be substantially more expensive than the courses offered by commercial training facilities for more standard packages; this is because the smaller market for library software increases the cost to the vendor of providing training services.

Libraries that cannot afford the expense of contracting with the vendor for training services may be able to learn the system "on-the-fly," assuming that the system has sufficient accompanying documentation (and that the documentation is comprehensible—which is not always the case). In these situations, a "train the trainer" approach may make sense. One or more employees can work through the documentation and tutorials until they feel comfortable with the operation of the system; they can then train other employees in a more structured setting.

Training for public access operations

Training issues become most complex for libraries when microcomputers will be used for public access activities—either in the searching of electronic information sources, or in the use of commercial and educational software programs. Not only must training be provided to staff, to the level that they are able to trouble-shoot the machines and provide assistance to patrons; in addition, training for patrons will also be necessary. Both requirements are discussed below.

Staff training

If staff members will need to supervise the use of public access microcomputers, additional training will be required. It will be necessary for these employees to have a greater understanding of the workings of the microcomputer—its hardware and its software—in order for them to provide assistance to patrons using the equipment and applications. In general, those who support a microcomputer system will always need more training than those who need only to use that system.

The additional training will fall into two primary areas. The first is the area of developing training and documentation skills. Library staff members responsible for the management of a public access area will need to be able to assist patrons and write useful documentation. These issues are discussed in more detail in Chapter 9.

The second area of importance, as noted earlier, is the development of more detailed knowledge about the specific hardware and software components of the system. A class on diagnosing and maintaining microcomputer hardware would be an excellent investment for those staff members who will have primary responsibility for the public access machines.

Patron training

When public access microcomputers are provided in a library, the issue of computer training for library patrons becomes critical. The library will need to determine to what extent it can provide training to users. Although the task of putting on training classes in the library can raise financial and staffing problems, it is important for libraries to consider this option in light of the growing need for computer skills as a component of literacy in today's business world.

If the library does choose to offer basic training in computer use, staff training again becomes a factor. It may be desirable to hire a staff person with computer background to take responsibility for the planning and presentation of training classes, as well as the preparation of supplementary documentation, and even the day-to-day operations of the public access facility.

Another issue that can arise if the library chooses to offer classes is that of software copyright. Because the standard licensing agreement for commercial software packages restricts use of that package to one computer, arrangements for site licenses or special permission to run the software on multiple machines must be made with the publisher of the software. Many software publishers will allow special arrangements for educational institutions, and libraries may be able to negotiate similar terms for training purposes.

Chapter 9

Keeping It Running

Now that the library has its microcomputers in place, it is essential that the job of microcomputer manager be assigned to one of the library staff members. This can be a full-time job if the number of microcomputers is large, or if the library intends to maintain regular public access to the computers. If the number of installed microcomputers is small, and the application load is light, management of the facility could be one part of the job of a staff member with other responsibilities. It is crucial, however, that the responsibility for management of the computer resources be assigned to a specific person; this will keep essential but often mundane tasks from falling by the wayside.

In order to maintain the usefulness of microcomputer equipment, it is necessary for the microcomputer manager to keep track of a variety of topics, ranging from the current availability of new software programs and hardware components to the implementation and enforcement of library software and computer use policies. Some of the challenges facing the microcomputer manager are discussed in this chapter; each library, however, will probably find that its environment has spawned a host of additional issues to address. This is merely a starting point.

Staff responsibilities

Assigning primary responsibility for the operations of the microcomputers to a single staff member is particularly useful in public access facilities, but holds true for administrative and library-specific automation as well. In his column in *Library Journal*, Robert M. Mason wrote:

> A good many libraries have discovered that the appointment of a computer coordinator makes their computer operations more effective. The coordinator, who may have additional responsibilities beyond those related to the microcomputer activities, serves as a central node in what may be a network of individuals whose responsibilities and activities involve the computer. . . . The coordinator maintains necessary records of usage, maintains supplies, and recommends modifications to operational procedures. As the number of micros increases, the coordinator may be responsible for supervising or coordinating the activities of other individuals.[8]

The assignment of a single individual as a coordinator or manager of the microcomputer facility is essential. It ensures that information will be received and recorded at a central point, and reduces the chance that necessary activities will be neglected or duplicated.

In a public access facility, the need for dedicated personnel becomes more important. In order to ensure the security of the computer components, it is necessary to have the computers supervised at all times. For this type of routine supervision, non-professional staff can certainly be utilized. However, patrons using public access computers will often encounter problems with or have questions about the hardware and software. For this reason, having a staff member available at all times who has been trained in the use and maintenance of the computers is important.

---

[8]Mason, Robert M. "The micro manager." *Library Journal*, v. 109, Apr. 15, 1984: 794-795.

Many libraries find that staffing a public access microcomputer center takes far more staff time than they had originally anticipated. This type of surprise can be minimized in the planning process when other libraries are contacted; their experiences can serve as a guide to proper planning for staff responsibilities.

Setting policies

In any automated environment, it is necessary to implement policies regarding use of computer equipment and software. Some of these policies will relate to administrative issues such as purchasing and maintenance; others will pertain to legal issues of copyright and piracy; still others will have to do with the library's responsibilities toward its patrons in the area of public access microcomputing and/or online searching.

Purchasing

Almost as soon as a library purchases a roomful of new computers, the equipment becomes obsolete. Even if the computers are considered state-of-the-art, users will immediately identify needs for new peripherals or other enhancements. These requests, whether they come from staff or patrons, can best be dealt with if procedures have been established for the request and purchase of new equipment and software.

One of the best ways to manage the onslaught of requests for additions and enhancements to the system is by providing a standard request form. The form should include, at the minimum, the following items:

- The name of the person making the request;

- Where the person can be contacted during the day (especially important if patrons will be submitting requests);

- The item being requested, with as much technical detail (including brand names and model numbers) as possible;

- Information on vendors of the item described, if known; and

•The reason for the request.

This form can then be reviewed by the person managing the facility. If the request appears to have merit, it can be researched further. Information that can then be added by the manager are:

•Citations to any literature found on the item requested;

•Vendors contacted that carry the item;

•The range of prices for the item (or for similar items, if it is available from a range of manufacturers); and

•Recommendation on whether or not to purchase.

If the recommendation is to purchase, the form can then be used as part of the justification process in procuring funds for the purchase. With this type of documentation, it is also possible to avoid duplicating research on items requested more than once, particularly if the decision not to purchase was based on an incompatibility or other problem unearthed in the course of the research.

Software copyright

The legal issues and responsibilities associated with the purchase and use of copyrighted software are important for all computer users; they are especially important for libraries and other environments where software is made available for short periods of time to a large and/or changeable group of potential users.

Most commercial software packages are licensed, rather than being sold outright. This licensing allows the manufacturer to maintain control over the distribution of the program, while granting the purchaser (or licensee) certain specific rights regarding its use. Unfortunately, many computer users are either unaware of the restrictions associated with their software licenses, or choose not to abide by the terms of the licensing agreement.

Although all licensing agreements vary slightly, most carry the same general restrictions and rights. They grant the purchaser of the program the right to use the software on one microcomputer at any given point in time, and prohibit the copying or distribution of the program to others. In some cases, the right to make a single copy for backup purposes is granted; even when it is not, no real legal risk is incurred by making archival copies that will be stored elsewhere, as long as the archival copy is *only* used if the original becomes lost or damaged. The right to transfer ownership of the program to another individual is also often included; this generally requires that the publisher be notified of the change in ownership, and that the original owner not retain a copy of the software.

Any library using microcomputer software needs to abide by the legal restrictions associated with the software license. This means that each microcomputer on which software will be used must have its own copy of the program.

There are variations on licensing agreements for software, and libraries may be able to arrange with software publishers for customized agreements. When an organization will be using a large number of copies of a given package, publishers will sometimes be willing to provide site licenses that allow unlimited use of the program on microcomputers within the company or institution (these site license agreements were also discussed in Chapter 6, under "Software costs").

Illegal copying of software (also known as "piracy") has become all too common today. It results in lost revenues in the millions of dollars for major software publishers. In the long run, it results in higher prices for software, as developers and publishers attempt to recoup the lost revenues through increased per unit prices. It also puts an organization at risk for copyright infringement lawsuits; the Software Publishers Association has begun prosecuting organizations that have flagrantly violated the terms of their licensing agreements. Even without the risk of legal retribution, however, libraries have a responsibility to their users to uphold principles of copyright and intellectual property.

Public access policies

In order to ensure that library microcomputer hardware and software will be used but not abused by patrons, certain restrictions should be imposed on prospective users of a public access computing facility.

These restrictions will need to cover a range of issues that relate to use of the microcomputers and software.

Training

One of the first issues to be addressed is that of training requirements. Although microcomputers are becoming easier to use all the time, they are not yet truly intuitive systems. A user with no knowledge of or training in microcomputer basics is quite capable of doing serious damage to a computer. It may therefore be necessary to require that patrons have a certain level of competence in microcomputer operations before they are allowed unsupervised access to the machines.

If access to the library's computers is limited to those with a basic understanding of the technology, some questions regarding literacy training and access to information must be confronted:

- Does the library have a responsibility to provide instruction to those patrons who do not meet these entry-level requirements?

- If so, would the classes be hands-on, or general in their approach?

- Where would the classes be held—in the library, or at an outside facility (e.g., a community college, computer center, or commercial training center)?

- Would a fee be charged for the class?

The last question, regarding a fee for instruction, is a particularly volatile one. The "fee vs. free" debate over charging for library services has yet to be resolved. As the role of the microcomputer in the library grows, this issue will only grow in importance; the cost of microcomputer equipment and the information services that the computers allow us to access will force all libraries into a serious consideration of this question.

These questions should all be considered and answered before the public access facility is made available to the public; information regarding training requirements and availability will need to be made available as soon as the facility opens.

Scheduling

Most libraries will find that the demand for use of their public access microcomputers often exceeds the available supply. In order to ensure that access to the computers is equitable, certain restrictions on use and scheduling of the computer resources should be put into place.

One method for limiting use that can be effective is to provide sign-up sheets with one-hour blocks of time for each of the available microcomputers. These sheets can be made available on a weekly or monthly basis. Patrons who have registered to use the microcomputers (see the section below on user registration) can then sign up for a set number of hour-long blocks. The number allowed per individual will vary based on the number of computers available, the type of applications being used on the computers, and the level of demand for this service.

User registration

When the public access facility opens to the public, a procedure will need to be implemented that will provide prospective users with all the necessary information regarding use of the computers. This information should include:

- A description of the available equipment and software;

- Hours the facility will be open;

- Any training requirements for users;

- Information on available training classes;

- An explanation of applicable copyright law and the concept of software piracy;

- General rules and regulations governing use of the facility, including preventive maintenance issues such as prohibition of food and drink, and cautions about magnetic media;

- Scheduling policies; and

- Penalties for violation of any facility rules or policies.

If this information is presented clearly when a patron first inquires about use of the facility, later misunderstandings and frustrations can be avoided. There are two excellent methods for distributing the information. First, it can be sent out in flyer form, as a method of publicizing the library's new services. Second, the policies can (and should) be restated on a registration sheet that all users of the facility must complete before they can have access to the computers.

Software circulation

Libraries with public access microcomputers face a decision as to how to circulate software packages. Some libraries choose to limit circulation to internal use on library microcomputers; others make a decision to allow software to circulate for home use. In either case, policies need to be established to ensure the safety of the program, as well as to guard against the spread of computer viruses, and to protect the library from copyright infringement liability.

Software that will be used only within the library on public access microcomputers can be more easily controlled. If it will be run from floppy diskettes, the circulating diskette should be a copy of the original; the original diskette should be stored in a safe (preferably off-site) location, and used only to make a new duplicate if the circulating copy is lost or stolen.

Diskettes that circulate—even if only within the library—should be labelled uniquely, so as to prevent patrons from accidentally or intentionally switching their own diskettes for the library's. They should also be write-protected, so that the program files are not overwritten or deleted, and to avoid infection of the application diskette with virus or worm programs.

It would be ideal if patrons could be prevented from using their own diskettes on library computers; this would limit the risk of infection, and would make it far more difficult for users to make pirated copies of library software. However, if patrons are to be able to save their own data files—whether they are text files of downloaded online searches, or documents created in an application program—they will need to put those files on their own diskettes. The resulting risk of infection and software piracy will need to be considered by the microcomputer facility manager. Information on how to prevent the spread of computer viruses and other harmful programs onto library microcomputers is provided in the section of Chapter 11 entitled "Disks and stored data files." In a public access environment, the risk of accidental or even intentional infection is very high, and it is important for library microcomputer managers to be well-informed about this threat.

Software piracy

Even when the library's computers are protected from infection, another risk associated with public-access computers remains. When expensive application programs are made available to computer users who might not wish to purchase them, the temptation to make an illegal copy is great. There are two approaches that need to be taken to prevent the use of the library's public access facility as a piracy center. The first is that of educating the users. Many computer users are unaware of the copyright restrictions associated with software programs, and make copies without realizing that they are violating copyright law. An excellent method for making library computer users aware of the restrictions on copying software is to include a statement providing this information on the user registration sheet that was discussed above.

Placing this information on a registration sheet signed by the patron ties into the second approach for ensuring cooperation, which is enforcement. In addition to the general information on why copying is not permitted, a statement could be included that indicates the user has read and understands the copying policy. Violation of this rule could result in a warning and/or suspension of computer use privileges.

Record-keeping procedures

In any microcomputer facility, a variety of records need to be kept regarding location, condition, and usage of the equipment. These records can be used for everything from calculating depreciation on capital equipment to implementing an appropriate schedule of preventive maintenance. They are also important for justification of additional purchases for or upgrades to the current system, enabling the manager to determine whether existing equipment can meet new needs, or whether additional purchases should be made.

These records, for the most part, fall into two primary categories. The first, inventory, includes detailed information on the type and location of all equipment and software. The second area is trouble-shooting and maintenance; it is discussed briefly below, and is also touched upon in Chapters 12 and 13.

Inventory

In the early days of computers, there was little risk of an employee or user misplacing or stealing a piece of a computer system; the equipment filled entire buildings, and were often immovable. In the microcomputer world, however, it is all too easy for pieces of expensive equipment to disappear, and it is essential for library microcomputer managers to keep track of all hardware and software owned by the library.

A manager taking over an already established facility will have a more difficult time creating a complete inventory of microcomputer equipment than a manager involved in the original purchase and installation of the equipment. The former has the burden of locating the equipment and tracking down old invoices and repair records—a task that, in a large microcomputer installation, can be formidable. The latter has the opportunity to record most of the necessary information for inventory and record-keeping purposes when the equipment is first purchased.

Ideally, an inventory system will consist of two parts. The first is a simple filing system, which should include original invoices, warranty information, and copies of any registration materials sent in to the manufacturer. The second is a database (or notebook) of individual workstation configurations, with references back to the paper files. The reason for maintaining the information grouped by workstation is that the interaction of components can be critical, particularly in trouble-shooting or purchasing situations.

The record-keeping needs of individual libraries will drive the design of the inventory system. Smaller libraries may not need to automate any part of their system, whereas larger libraries may need a more complex database that allows for a range of reports to be output. All libraries, however, will benefit from a reliable and up-to-date inventory of their microcomputer systems.

Once the system has been implemented, it is also vital that staff members be assigned the responsibility for regularly checking the inventory lists against the actual configurations, and recording or reporting any changes or discrepancies.

Trouble-shooting and maintenance

Closely associated with the inventory are the records of trouble-shooting and maintenance calls. As is discussed in Chapter 12, it is important to designate a central individual or telephone number for users to contact when they experience problems with their microcomputers. When a request for assistance is made, it needs to be recorded in a central log book. This log book will be an excellent tool for identifying recurring problems with the microcomputer facility, and identifying solutions such as additional training or changes in software configurations.

A link should be maintained between the problem reports and the inventory; some method for recording maintenance done on a given piece of equipment should exist so that chronic problems or inadequate repairs can be spotted and addressed.

Chapter 10

Introduction to Maintaining Microcomputer Facilities in Libraries

Once a manager has finally evaluated, purchased, and installed the microcomputers, trained the staff in their use, publicized the newly automated facility, and started to use the long-awaited machines, the job is only partially complete. Although personal computers are truly marvelous products of modern engineering, they are far from infallible. It won't be long, alas, before things start to go wrong. As the author of an article in the October 1983 issue of *PC Magazine* said:

> Someday, computers will be foolproof. But by then we'll all be dust settling onto some future user's hyperspace drive. Laurel and Hardy would have had a field day with today's systems. It's pretty easy to visualize the boys behind a mountain of smoking, broken computer rubble while Stan screws up his face and bawls and Ollie stares dejectedly into the lens and plays with his tie.[9]

---

[9]Somerson, Paul. "Goblins, gremlins, & glitches." *PC Magazine,* v. 2, Oct. 1983: 112-129.

You may well find yourself feeling like Stan or Ollie as you look at a monitor display that bears a distinct resemblance to your television set tuned to a non-broadcasting channel, or engage in a conversation with your repair shop that sounds a bit too much like the "Who's on first?" routine for comfort. It is realistic to expect a certain level of downtime, but careful planning can minimize both its occurrence and its impact on library operations. When all else fails, though—as it's likely to do at times—a sense of humor will be the most effective tool available.

Maintaining a microcomputer facility involves more than simply signing a repair contract and hoping for the best. Maintenance of a computer system is a full-time endeavor in and of itself. There are a number of precautions, however, that can be taken to ensure that the equipment is treated properly and repaired effectively. Some of these tasks are simply common sense measures—keeping the work areas clean and organized, for example. Others require more extensive knowledge—from trouble-shooting methods for malfunctioning modems to cleaning keyboards with cans of compressed air.

This portion of the book will provide the basic information a microcomputer facility manager needs to keep the system running smoothly. The first chapter provides definitions of the two primary types of maintenance that microcomputers require—preventive and responsive—and how these types of maintenance affect the management of the microcomputer facility.

Microcomputer maintenance is all too often thought of as the series of steps one must take when a piece of equipment fails to operate properly. In fact, however, those steps are merely responsive maintenance, and constitute only one part of the broader area of microcomputer maintenance. Responsive maintenance includes such issues as trouble-shooting routines, service contracts, and work performed by in-house service technicians. This type of maintenance is unavoidable for any computer, but is likely to be a regular necessity for heavily used microcomputers in public access areas.

It is possible to lessen the need for regular (and often quite expensive) maintenance on your computers by instituting a program of preventive maintenance. Although it is discussed far less in microcomputer literature, preventive maintenance can be the most important kind of maintenance you perform. A proper routine of preventive maintenance can save the library a great deal of money, since well cared for equipment will be less likely to fail, and will therefore generate far lower costs for responsive maintenance.

This section of the book addresses the general issues of preventive and responsive maintenance, and explains how to set up routines that will keep your systems running as smoothly as possible, and minimize the trauma of downed machines and lost data. Indeed, routines are the key to effective maintenance; by instituting standard procedures and making individual staff members responsible for carrying out these procedures, an effective manager will be able to keep the microcomputers running more reliably.

Chapter 11

Preventive Maintenance

Little information currently exists on preventive maintenance for microcomputers. The few pieces that have been written have appeared sporadically in personal computing magazines, and fail to address many of the library-specific issues that library and information center managers must face, particularly when public access machines are installed. One reason for the lack of literature in this area is the reluctance on the part of many PC owners to take the time to perform basic preventive maintenance tasks. Bill Machrone, now the editor of PC *Magazine*, began one article:

> Sure there's information on preventive maintenance in [the literature], but even if it did any good, would you actually do it? . . . There are two schools of thought here. One says to spend much time and trouble puttering around trying to forestall future grief. The other says to spend that time actually using your machine and to deal with problems when and where they arise. The latter is a default.[10]

Can most libraries, however, *afford* that default? The research organization IDC (International Data Corporation) has found that a full

---

[10]Machrone, Bill. "Run it till it breaks." *PC Magazine*, v. 2, Oct. 1983: 136-139.

two-thirds of the lifetime cost of a personal computer can be spent on maintenance and repair.[11] That doesn't include the cost of lost time and data, nor the lost faith on the part of both patrons and staff in the ability of the computers to serve as effective tools. For the small expenditure of time and money that a good preventive maintenance routine requires, managers can save themselves immeasurable amounts of lost time and productivity.

Most preventive maintenance tasks are designed to keep computer hardware running smoothly. However, preventive maintenance should include more than the tending of the mechanical parts of the system. It is also important to maintain safeguards for your software and data, on whatever media they are stored; floppy diskettes, hard drives, optical disks, CD-ROM discs, magnetic tapes, and other storage media all have their pitfalls, and it is dangerous to ever take data for granted. Much of this section is devoted to hardware issues; however, there is also some discussion of ways to protect your more ephemeral disk-based software and data.

Many non-technical managers find that computer equipment can be quite mystifying; often the documentation accompanying a new computer system or peripheral equipment is unintelligible, and the experts writing the manuals can seem to be speaking a foreign language. In reality, however, it is not at all difficult to build a basic understanding of the components of a microcomputer and how they work. Some basic concepts are touched upon in this chapter and in Chapter 12, which covers responsive maintenance issues. Managers of automated facilities, or those planning to introduce computers into their workplaces, ought to invest in at least one basic reference book on the computer system they select for their environment. A list of some of the more comprehensive and readable guides is included in Appendix B.

---

[11]Quoted in: "A dollop of prevention, a pinch of repair," by Carol Olsen Day. *P C Magazine*, v. 5, June 10, 1985: 213-219.

Remember that the most important concept to remember for successful preventive maintenance is that of *routine*. Preventive maintenance must be done regularly in order to be effective. It is vital that a regular schedule be created for these tasks, and that specific individuals are charged with responsibility for completion of the tasks. Without this type of structured routine, it is unlikely that preventive maintenance activities will be completed often enough to have an impact on the reliability or longevity of the computers. In addition, the establishment of rules regarding use of the computers and their environment, along with the vigilant enforcement of those rules, can have a dramatic effect upon the effectiveness of preventive maintenance activities.

What follow are the specific preventive maintenance tasks that your microcomputer equipment requires. The various components of your system, ranging from the environment in which it is contained to the data files that it produces, are addressed individually, with basic preventive measures given first, and the options for responsive maintenance given second.

Tools

There are a number of tools that should be kept on hand for basic preventive maintenance tasks on microcomputer hardware. Unlike the tool kits available from computer suppliers for responsive maintenance tasks, preventive maintenance tool kits must be assembled by the user. The table on the next page includes a list of these tools and their functions. Most of these tools should be available from local office or computer supply stores. If not, a number of library supply companies stock these products. The cost of these items will be very low, and the benefits gained by using them regularly in a preventive maintenance program will more than offset the expense.

TOOLS FOR BASIC PREVENTIVE MAINTENANCE

Flashlight	Illumination
Compressed air	Removing dust from keyboard and interior of printer
Isopropyl alcohol & foam or cotton swabs	Removing buildup from disk drives
Pencil eraser or special swabs	Cleaning contacts on boards
Lint-free cloths	General cleaning
Glass cleaner	Cleaning monitor (NOTE: some screens with coatings may need special cleaners; consult manual)
Vacuum cleaner	Removing dust and dirt
Diagnostic disks	Checking disk drives

Environment

The physical environment housing your microcomputers is one of the most ignored and, simultaneously, most important factors in the health and longevity of your computer equipment. A great number of potential computer hazards lurk in most office and library environments, and all too often these hazards go unrecognized and uncorrected. Many environmental issues can be resolved in the planning stages of microcomputer installation—for instance, the quality of the electrical wiring and outlets in the work area, and the problems of high heat and humidity during summer months. If these areas have not been addressed during the initial preparation for your computer equipment, they should be given immediate attention.

Electrical power

The first environmental factor to consider is that of power supply. As mentioned in Section One of this book, in Chapter 4: System Requirements, and in Chapter 7: Purchase and Installation, a strong and steady electrical power supply as well as fully grounded electrical outlets are essential for a safe computing area.

The most common power-related problems tend to be "surges" and "spikes" of electrical power through the lines that feed the computer. If the library's computers are sharing a circuit with any high-drain equipment—ranging from a vacuum cleaner to a PA system—there is a risk of brief power drains whenever that equipment is turned on. These fluctuations in power can cause damage not only to the magnetic media storing data, but also to the machinery in the microcomputers and peripheral equipment. The easiest protection against this type of mishap is a surge suppressor. This is a multi-outlet device which plugs into a grounded electrical outlet, and serves as a safe power strip for all the computer components. It screens out the brief fluctuations in power that can occur from time to time, and can be instrumental in preventing innumerable disk crashes and destruction of valuable components. Surge suppressors are relatively inexpensive, though they can range in cost and quality, and can be found in almost any office or computer supply store.

If the library's computers are used to store large amounts of difficult to replace or restore data (for example, circulation records or downloaded online searches), it might be wise to consider an investment in an uninterruptible power supply (UPS). This piece of equipment monitors the power supply to the computer; when it detects a power outage, it will immediately compensate with sufficient battery-generated power to keep the system safe while data is saved and the equipment is shut down. These uninterruptible power supplies can range in price from a few hundred to over one thousand dollars; the peace of mind they provide, however, may well be worth this expense if the data on your microcomputers cannot be backed up regularly enough to protect you in power outage situations. (For more information on data backups, see the section on preventive maintenance for software and stored data files that appears later in this chapter.)

Air quality

The next factor to be considered in an inspection of environmental hazards is air quality. If the local climate tends toward high summer heat and humidity levels, air conditioning is essential for a safe operating environment. Computer components can overheat easily, and this tendency is exacerbated by a warm or damp environment. It is important to determine whether the microcomputers being used have internal fans built in; if they do not, consider installing them. Many suppliers of computer accessories carry air cooling systems for a variety of computers. Watch for signs of overheating, particularly during the summer months. Often the screen display is the first to go, and will show signs of flickering or distortion before permanent damage is done. Some hard drives will show persistent error messages when the system overheats. Any sign of malfunction on a hot day should be a warning to turn the system off for a while and let it cool down. If the problems recur, the malfunctioning component(s) should be checked for damage. If the problems do not recur, the machine should be watched carefully to ensure that it does not overheat.

Clean air is as important to computer health as cool air. Libraries in which dust is a regular problem should consider investment in covers for all computer components to be used when the systems are not in use. These covers, available from most computer suppliers, help prevent the accumulation of damaging dust and debris inside the components.

Another airborne hazard is smoke, particularly tobacco smoke. Smoking should be prohibited in any areas containing computer equipment. Not only does the smoke carry ash that can penetrate into the crevices of the computer, it also carries tar, which is attracted to electrically charged surfaces such as those inside the computer components. The tar can collect on the contacts inside the computer, leading to keyboard failures and processing errors.

Static electricity

Once the air has finally been made cool, clean, and dry, another hazard needs to be addressed: static electricity. Static at its most harmless can freeze a screen display, forcing a user to restart the machine; this often results in loss of data. Static at its most dangerous can do serious damage to—or even destroy—internal boards, disk drives, and other components. There are a number of products available that will decrease the risk of damage by static charge. Mats can be purchased for placement under the chairs and tables around the computer; these will help prevent static from building up through constant contact with a carpeted floor. Pads can be purchased which sit next to or in front of a keyboard; users touch these pads to discharge static from their bodies before they make physical contact with the computers. Finally, there are anti-static sprays available for use in minimizing static risks; these sprays help neutralize charges that have built up on surfaces around the computers, and create a barrier that inhibits static buildup.

Spills

Another environmental enemy of the computer is the food and drink so often placed next to keyboards and disks. The crumbs from the food are bad enough, and can easily fall between the keys of the keyboard, preventing contact or causing stickiness when the keys are depressed. It is the liquids, however, that present one of the most common and dangerous threats to the keyboard's health. A carelessly spilled cup of coffee or can of soda can do irreparable damage to the circuits inside the keyboards. Although spill damage can be wiped clean if the keyboard is disassembled, if the drink contained sugar, it is likely to permanently corrode the sensitive contacts on the internal circuit boards, and will often require a complete replacement of the keyboard.

In a library microcomputer user group newsletter that was distributed over a year ago, the following quote appeared:

> Nobody wants to stay late at school doing computer tasks when there's the alternative of doing these very same things in the comfort of one's own home, with coffee, cigarettes, snacks, TV, or whatever your secret vice, close at hand.

What a librarian does in the privacy of his or her own home is, of course, his or her own business. Anyone planning to reduce their maintenance costs on a computer, however, would be best advised keeping most of the "secret vices" mentioned above away from their expensive equipment.

Hardware

The information provided above regarding environmental maintenance is, for the most part, concerned with one-time installation of equipment and procedures. What follows in this section on hardware concerns the day-to-day work that must be done regularly in order to ensure the smooth operation of the computers. Just as plants must be watered and floors must be swept, so must these routine tasks be performed in order to protect the investment made in microcomputer equipment. These tasks can be ideal for assignment to volunteer workers in the library or to clerical help. Ideally, a master schedule of preventive maintenance tasks should be created, and the individual tasks assigned to specific workers. This eliminates the primary reason why preventive maintenance tasks are not performed in so many computer installations; no one has been charged with specific responsibility for the activities. Once the tasks have been defined, scheduled, and assigned, the routines will quickly fall into place.

One thing to keep in mind before performing any of the maintenance tasks described below: always turn off *and* unplug all components before beginning work. A substantial level of electrical current runs through most microcomputer equipment, even when the system is not switched on. Unplugging the components protects both the system and the worker.

Display monitor

As the component that receives the most daily scrutiny, the monitor is the first item in a microcomputer system to show immediate signs of neglect. The magnetic components inside the monitor impart a slight charge to the glass of the screen, and this charge tends to attract a great deal of airborne dust. In addition, users have a tendency to point to items on the screen, and in the process they leave behind slight traces of oil and dirt from their fingertips. This combination of factors results in a regular need to clean the glass of the monitor's screen, particularly in a public access computer facility. Although most monitor screens can be cleaned with standard household glass cleaners, there are some screens which have had special coatings applied to them. Before cleaning a screen with an anti-glare coating, or one that is touch-sensitive, be sure to consult the owners' manual for any special cleaning instructions; if no documentation is available, and the manufacturer and vendor are unable to make recommendations, a safe alternative is a soft, lint-free cloth that can be used to wipe the surface without the use of a liquid cleaning agent.

Once a cleaner has been selected, appropriate paper towels or cloths should be obtained. Ideally, the material used to wipe the screen should be soft and as lint-free as possible. The cleaner should never be sprayed directly onto the screen; instead, it should be applied to the cloth or paper towel, and then wiped onto the screen. This prevents excess cleaner from dripping down the glass into the monitor, creating possible problems with the circuitry.

The schedule for cleaning a monitor screen will vary, and will be affected by such factors as the level of dust in the air, and the degree to which users make direct contact with the screen. A regular schedule for cleaning can be established by evaluating the condition of the screen on a regular basis, and recording the frequency with which cleaning is required. Once a pattern has been established, a regular schedule can be defined.

Monitors can also be adversely affected by prolonged display of a single, unchanging screen (for example, an introductory menu or welcoming display). If a single image is projected onto the screen for long periods of time, the image can become "burned in" to the screen itself, and the ghost of that image will remain visible during all operations. This burn-in cannot be repaired, and it is therefore necessary to take precautions to avoid this type of prolonged display.

One of the best methods for avoiding screen burn-in is the use of a screen-save program. These programs keep track of computer activity, and will blank the screen (or project a changing pattern) when no activity is detected after a given period of time. Some monitors are shipped with screen saver programs, and when this occurs, it is usually best to use the program included. In particular, monitors using Hercules graphics cards *must* use the save function in the graphics utility package accompanying the graphics card; use of other screen savers with the Hercules graphics card can cause a number of problems in operation of the monitor. It is possible to purchase screen savers from commercial software publishers, as well as to download public domain or shareware versions from bulletin board systems.

It is possible to take measures to prevent screen burn-in without installing a screen-saver program. If the monitor is turned off or the brightness is turned all the way down when the computer is not in use, no image will appear on the screen and the risk of burn-in will be eliminated. This does, however, require regular monitoring of all computers to ensure that those not in use have been turned off or down. In addition, this can disconcert users who do not realize that the screen has been intentionally disabled.

Keyboard

The keyboard is most at risk from environmental hazards such as those mentioned in preceding sections: dust, food, and drinks. Even when precautions are taken against these threats, however, there are activities that can be undertaken to improve the performance and extend the life expectancy of any keyboard.

Keyboards that are used heavily, particularly those used for public access, tend to accumulate a great deal of dirt on the surface of the keys themselves, making them sticky and unpleasant to the touch. This can be remedied with standard household cleaning liquids. The liquid should be applied to a cotton swab, or to the end of a paper towel, which can then be used to gently wipe the surface of the keys. Like all cleaning activities, this should be done when the computer is turned off and unplugged, so it should be possible to press the keys down while the cleaning is done. Although keeping the keytops clean is unlikely to affect the operation of the keyboard, it will certainly make use of the computer far more pleasant.

The accumulation of dust underneath and between the keys, however, does pose a threat to the keyboard's performance. In order to keep the keyboard functioning properly, it is necessary to regularly clean dust and dirt out from inside the keyboard. The dust can block the contacts, resulting in nonfunctional or erratically functioning keys. One of the best ways to combat dust buildup is with compressed air, which is available from both camera and computer supply stores. The air comes in a spray can, which directs a tightly focused stream of clean air that will blow dust out from normally inaccessible areas. In environments where dust is a major problem, it may also be helpful to invest in a small vacuum, also available from computer supply stores. If a vacuum is used, be sure *not* to reverse the air stream in order to duplicate the effect of compressed air. Because this does not utilize sterile air, it will simply blow more dust into the keyboard, exacerbating rather than relieving problems.

Floppy disk drives

The issue of disk drive cleaning has stirred up controversy in many microcomputer facilities. Disk drive cleaners work by abrading the drive heads with a cleaning solution that has been applied to a rough surface. This removes oxides and contaminants that can interfere with the drive head's ability to make contact with the disk itself. Although manufacturers of disk drives and disk drive cleaning materials will often instruct users to clean the drives on a weekly or monthly basis, many computer experts feel that cleaning the drives that often is likely to cause more harm than good. Overuse of these cleaners can result in permanent damage to the drive head. Common wisdom is to clean the drives approximately twice a year. This will help keep material from building up on the drive heads, but will cut down on unnecessary abrading of the heads and possible damage to the drive.

It is also advisable to occasionally run a diagnostic program on the drives that will check their speed and alignment. These programs can be obtained from computer supply houses and computer equipment vendors. Although it is not possible to take measures to prevent the gradual changes in a drive's accuracy, it is possible to identify problems before they begin causing problems with data. If these programs are run, they should be used after the drives have been cleaned; like the cleaning, diagnostics need not be done more than twice a year.

Hard disk drives

Hard drives are seldom mentioned in the literature on preventive maintenance; unfortunately, they generally get attention only after they have crashed, taking megabytes of data with them. There are however, precautions that can be taken before disaster strikes. In some cases, these procedures will improve the performance of the disk on a day-to-day basis; in other cases, they will actually extend the life of the disk, and can make it easier to recover data if the disk should crash.

One type of utility that should be run regularly on a hard disk is called a "defragmenter." It is a software program that reads the data on a hard disk, and moves it around so that all data files consist of contiguous clusters on the disk. If a defragmenting program is not run often enough, data files can end up spread out across an entire disk. This slows the drive down during disk access, and results in slower performance from the computer. An added advantage to running these programs is that they can identify bad sectors on the hard drive, and will often "lock out" those areas that could be unsafe for data. Defragmenting programs are often included in packages of hard disk utilities like PC Tools Deluxe and Norton Utilities for IBM compatibles, and Symantec Utilities for the Macintosh and Mac Tools Deluxe.

Another problem that can arise on hard drives in IBM-compatible computers is a gradual degradation of the disk's low-level formatting and interleave ratio. There is a program available called SpinRite, which allows users to reset interleave ratios and redo the low-level formatting of a hard drive, *without* losing data from the drive in the process. This is an excellent addition to any preventive maintenance toolkit.

Modem

For the most part, modems require very little attention in the way of preventive maintenance. The exception to this is in the area of electrical hazards. Modem circuitry is very vulnerable to damage from surges of electrical current, and this threat presents itself through two channels. The first, and most obvious, is the power supply for the modem. For an external modem, a surge suppressor for the power cord should be an effective safeguard; for an internal modem, a surge suppressor for the system unit will serve the same purpose. The second, and less obvious, threat to the modem comes from the telephone line itself. Although most telephone lines are equipped with some degree of electrical protection, this protection is not always sufficient. During an electrical storm, intense electrical charges from lightning can be sent across the telephone lines, resulting in serious damage to the internal circuitry of the modem. Some electrical surge suppressors do come equipped with jacks for modular telephones, and this can be an effective means of additional protection. The only guarantee of safety, however, comes from unplugging modem telephone lines from their jacks during electrical storms.

Printer

The printer is one of the most vulnerable components of a microcomputer system. The paper running through the printer creates dust, particularly in printers using pin-fed paper, and the ink from ribbons and cartridges can easily make mechanical parts sticky and non-functional. Since the printer often has more moving parts than any other piece of equipment in the system, the constant motion leads to more frequent breakdowns. Although it is not possible to prevent these problems completely, it is possible to slow the process and limit the number of repairs necessary by taking good care of the printer.

The most important thing that can be done to keep a printer functioning well is keeping it clean. The compressed air mentioned in the section on keyboards is also a useful tool for cleaning dust out of printers. Another valuable cleaning supply for printers is the solvent WD-40. Although this preparation is most often used as a lubricant, it can also be used to dissolve the residue of ink and labels that may adhere to the platen of the printer.

Also important in the preventive maintenance of printers is regular lubrication of mechanical parts. Although WD-40 can also be used to lubricate some printers, it is important to check the specific instructions in the printer manual to determine what type of lubrication should be used in that model. Printers vary substantially in their design and construction, and the manufacturer's guidelines should be followed carefully for this procedure.

Disks and stored data files

Disk-based information, like software and data files, is not generally mentioned in discussions of microcomputer maintenance. There are, however, a number of precautions that can be taken to avoid loss of valuable programs or information. Anything stored on a magnetic media, such as a floppy or hard disk or cassette tape, is surprisingly vulnerable to damage by any number of workplace hazards. These can include anything from cups of coffee to paper clip holders.

In addition, the advent of computer viruses—programs designed to destroy or corrupt data on hard disk drives without the user's knowledge or consent—have put library computing facilities, particularly those with public access computers, at great risk.

The first section below discusses specific maintenance tasks for magnetic media and files on disks, and provides information on how to safeguard data and programs from environmental hazards and human error. The second section covers the importance of instituting backup procedures, and describes several methods available for backing up disks. Finally, the third addresses methods for preventing the infection of disks and applications with dangerous virus programs. It is important to keep the safety of software and data in mind as maintenance routines are developed.

Maintenance tasks

The majority of microcomputers currently marketed use magnetic media as their primary format for data storage. Floppy disks of all kinds, hard drives, and cartridge or cassette tape drives are all types of of this media commonly associated with microcomputer technology. Although magnetic media offers the ability to easily read data from and write data to its surface, and provides an extremely cost-effective method for mass

126

storage, it is far from a foolproof method for data storage and retrieval. It is easy to think of data written to a computer disk as secure, but in reality that data can be lost in an instant unless precautions are taken to protect it.

Data on magnetic media is vulnerable to electrical charges, such as static electricity or power surges (both of which were discussed under the section "Environment" earlier in this chapter). It can also be threatened by any foreign magnetic charge, even from a source as benign as a paperclip holder. Some tips for protecting data stored on disks are detailed below.

- Don't use ball-point or other hard-tipped pens when labelling disks—the pens can damage the fragile media inside of the plastic cover. If the disk must be labelled directly, use a felt-tip pen. Ideally, the label should be filled out *before* it is affixed to the disk.

- Never touch the exposed surface of the disk inside the disk cover. The natural oils on your skin will stick to the magnetic media, and may result in errors when the computer attempts to read the data from the disk.

- Don't "bend, fold, spindle, or mutilate" the disk. Any crease on the disk surface can cause disks to become unreadable.

- Disks should never be placed in direct sunlight, or on a heat-generating surface. The disks will melt even more quickly than a vinyl record. If you've ever seen a library display of LPs that have been left out in the back-seat of a car, or on top of a radiator, you can begin to imagine the extent of the damage that could result to the disk.

- Keep disks away from magnetic fields of any kind. Magnetic fields can erase data from your disks, and data erased in this manner is unrecoverable. No magnets in your office, you say? You'd be surprised. Telephone bells, fluorescent lamp transformers, electric typewriters, computer printers, color TVs, even some desk accessories (paper clip holders and the clips used to hold papers over a keyboard are just two common culprits) can contain magnets that are capable of damaging your disks.

Even the best of efforts to protect disk- and tape-based data eventually fail, since magnetic media is by nature impermanent. If a disk should turn up as unreadable, there are some methods for attempting recovery of the data. These operations are detailed in Chapter 12, under the heading "Disks and stored data files."

For computers with hard drives, there are utilities available from commercial software publishers that will minimize the risk of data loss if a hard disk crash should occur. On IBM-compatible computers, PC Tools Deluxe has certain protection programs that will make data recovery more reliable after a crash. On Macintosh computers, both Symantec Utilities for the Macintosh and Mac Tools Deluxe offer this feature.

Backup procedures

Since disk failure is inevitable, backing up data is essential. On a system using only floppy diskettes, it is easy to keep copies of the diskettes with critical data files. On a system with a hard drive, the larger quantity of data to be backed up has resulted in a greater number of options for the backup process.

On the most basic level, a backup can consist simply of copies of critical data files that are put onto floppy diskettes on a regular basis and stored separately There are several drawbacks to this method. The first is that it is likely to result in a number of files being left off the backup set that might actually be critical to bringing the computer back up after a hard disk crash. For example, a user might not think to back up program files, assuming that they can always be restored from the original program diskettes; however, if the program has been customized for use on a particular configuration, reconstructing that configuration after a reinstallation can be a tedious and difficult process.

The next step up from simple file copying is the use of whatever backup program came with the computer's operating system. On IBM-compatible microcomputers, DOS includes a backup program called BACKUP. On the Macintosh, a utility called HD BACKUP is shipped on one of the utilities disks. Both of these programs provide what is called "incremental" backups of the hard disk. They allow the user to back up all or some of the hard disk to floppy diskettes on the first backup, and compress the data into single files on each diskette used. After the first backup is performed, subsequent backups can back up all files again, or can back up only the files that have been added or changed since the last backup was done. Although these utilities will do the job, their user interfaces are less than elegant, and the user has a very limited range of options in the backup process.

The third backup option is the use of commercial backup programs. These programs offer the user a wider range of options in determining which files and directories (or folders, on the Macintosh) will be backed up. If a high-capacity tape drive is being used for backup purposes, commercial products will often provide the capacity for unattended backup—the backup process can then take place during non-work hours and will not require the user to initiate the process.

Some computer managers will argue that keeping only one backup set is almost as risky as not keeping a backup at all. This is because one flaw in the backup set can often make the information unrecoverable, and because at least one set of backup data should always be kept in a remote location. Keeping two or more backup sets, and rotating among them, will result in a more secure backup process, and will allow the library to store at least one backup set off-site in case a fire or other building-wide disaster destroys the information on the computer system.

If a computer will be used to store data that has value to the library, ranging from circulation data to administrative records, it is essential that the information be backed up regularly. The growing risk of damage to or loss of data resulting from computer viruses makes regular backup procedures even more critical.

Virus prevention

There are two ways to prevent viruses[12] from infecting data and program files on disks. The first is to practice "safe computing." This involves never using software before its source has been verified,

---

[12]Technically, the term "virus" refers to a specific type of harmful program that replicates itself within a computer system. For the purposes of this book, however, the term will be used to encompass all types of harmful computer programs, including "worms" and "trojan horse" programs.

avoiding software that has been downloaded from an electronic bulletin board system (BBS), and limiting the exchange of data via floppy diskettes that is done with computers that are not located at the library.

In any environment, it is difficult to enforce these precautions; in a library with public access microcomputers, it is nearly impossible. And even when these measures *are* taken, it is still possible for a harmful computer program to sneak through. In some cases, viruses have actually been found on original program diskettes sent from commercial software packages, or even on new hard drives purchased from a vendor. Because the risk is so great, there are also more proactive methods for preventing computer infection.

For the IBM-PC and compatibles, one of the best resources available is a book titled *V.I.R.U.S. Protection: Vital Information Resources Under Siege*, by Pamela Kane. The book provides a comprehensive overview of the range of issues relating to data security on computers. It is accompanied by a diskette of virus prevention programs that can be installed onto an IBM-compatible microcomputer. Even users of other computer systems will find this book interesting in its treatment of the general issues of computer viruses and other threats to computer-based information.

For the Macintosh, there are a range of commercial and shareware software products that provide virus prevention functions. On the commercial side, Symantec Anti-virus utilities for the Macintosh (S.A.M.) and Virex both provide excellent and regularly updated protection. For those on a more limited budget, there are Virus Rx (produced by Apple Computer) and Disinfectant as stand-alone programs, and Vaccine, a program which loads when the computer is first turned on, and which stands guard against possible infections. The books *Encyclopedia Macintosh* and *The Macintosh Bible* provide some useful information on potential virus threats—and defenses against them—for the Macintosh environment.

Chapter 12

Responsive Maintenance

Despite our best efforts to keep micros running through regular preventive maintenance routines, even the most reliable of computers is bound to require some repairs from time to time. When the machines do fail, it is important to determine as specifically as possible what needs to be repaired or replaced. This information will aid in the decision as to what response is most appropriate. Some repairs are quite simple, and can be done easily by library staff who have had proper training. Other repairs will require the assistance of a trained repair technician. Even when the computer does need expert attention, it is important to give as much information as possible to the technician in order to keep the cost of the repairs as low as possible; a major component of the repair charge is often the time spent determining what has gone wrong.

Hardware

There are some general issues to take into consideration when addressing computer failure problems. The issues vary greatly depending on the various hardware and software components of your system, so individual sections have been devoted to each of the major system components in this chapter.

All microcomputer facilities should have a basic repair kit available for use by those library staff members who have been trained in troubleshooting activities. Basic PC maintenance kits can be purchased at many computer stores, as well as through mail-order equipment distributors. It is also possible to assemble your own kit by purchasing items not already owned to supplement existing tools. A list of essential items is shown in the table below.

TOOLS FOR BASIC RESPONSIVE MAINTENANCE

Screwdrivers:

1/4" flat blade	Loosening and tightening slotted screws on system unit & keyboard
1/8" flat blade	Loosening and tightening slotted screws on interface cables
small Phillips	Loosening and tightening other screws on and inside chassis
non-conductive	To loosen and tighten screws in an electrically charged environment

Pliers:

needle nose	To grip and/or bend small objects
standard	To grip and/or bend small objects, and to hold and turn small nuts

Wire strippers/cutters	To cut wire and strip insulation
Contact cleaner (aerosol)	To clean dirty or malfunctioning electrical contacts

Far more computer repair than most microcomputer users realize can be done outside of a computer repair shop; this is often because owners have insufficient knowledge of their systems. It is essential for microcomputer facility managers to have a basic working knowledge of the equipment they control. This enables the manager to quickly assess the scope of a problem when it occurs, and to choose the appropriate course of action, whether that involves having the unit serviced by a qualified technician, or simply making adjustments in-house. The best place for a beginner to start is with the manual for the system. Although many of these manuals are poorly written, and can present a challenge to the "non-technical" reader, they do provide an essential view of the individual components of the system.

A number of good comprehensive guides to microcomputer functions and repairs are available commercially. One of the best is Henry F. Beechhold's *The Plain English Repair & Maintenance Guide for IBM Personal Computers*, which provides both general tips on maintenance and specific technical information on the operation of the IBM-PC. Although a similar text for the Macintosh does not currently exist, the book *Encyclopedia Macintosh*, by Craig Danuloff and Deke McClelland provides a substantial amount of technical information on error codes and internal architecture that can be utilized by those interested in doing their own repair work. Similar books and pertinent journal articles appear in the maintenance bibliography in Appendix B.

Another option for library managers and/or staff members is a course in maintaining or repairing microcomputers. These courses are offered in many major metropolitan areas, and provide a comprehensive, hands-on overview of microcomputer hardware and troubleshooting methods. Most of these training programs are advertised through direct mail advertising, and it can be difficult to identify good courses from a single brochure. Find out from the companies offering the courses whether they can give the names of local companies that have sent employees to the course in question, so that references can be gathered.

Troubleshooting techniques

There are a number of steps that should be followed at the start of any microcomputer repair effort. Although they may seem simplistic, they often reveal a simple and inexpensive solution to what may have seemed a potentially devastating problem.

- Make sure that the power to the machine is turned on. This includes verifying that there is power coming from the outlet (try plugging in a small lamp or other appliance to check this), making sure that the power strip or surge suppressor has not been turned off, and checking that the power cord is securely connected at both ends.

• Ensure that all cables are securely connected; a loose connection can bring an entire system down.

• Are the components clean, or is there a visible film of dirt or dust? Cleaning the computer can often result in improved performance, since dirt and dust can prevent electrical contacts from working properly.

• If the computer came with a diagnostic diskette (most IBM-compatible computers do), boot the computer from this disk and run the programs included. The diagnostic programs are designed to identify the specific component of the computer that is functioning improperly.

If these routines do not result in a solution to the problem, the next step is to identify the specific component that is not functioning. One of the best ways to determine this is by using spare parts, either from a stock of parts maintained by the computer coordinator, or from another working microcomputer. There is, however, a risk involved in this sort of component swapping. In some cases, the malfunctioning equipment has somehow been damaged by a flaw in the system; in this case, a new, functioning piece of equipment could well be damaged in the same manner. For this reason, it is better to use spare parts from stock for this type of activity than to "cannibalize" another user's machine.

When the broken component has been identified, the material that follows in this chapter can be used to determine whether the repair can easily and safely be performed in-house, or whether a repair service should be contacted.

There are a few things to keep in mind when any internal repairs to computer equipment are attempted:

• Be sure there is a clean, flat surface on which to place the computer, with additional open space for components that have been removed;

• Use non-conductive tools, so as to limit the risk of static discharge onto sensitive parts; and

•Ensure that the person doing the work grounds his or herself before touching any components—a static discharge strip or mat nearby can help with this.

Processing unit, memory, and co-processor chips

If the computer appears to have a problem with its ability to process information—for example, if error messages or system crashes are appearing during use—the problem may well be related to the processing unit or memory. For the most part, these are *not* user-serviceable parts, and should be replaced or repaired only by a trained technician. There are, however, some exceptions to this rule.

If the memory or co-processor was installed in-house, it is likely that it can also be removed by the same individual. Sometimes memory or processing errors occur because a chip was not properly seated on the machine's motherboard. This type of problem can be solved by removing the chip from its socket, and then carefully reseating it.

Any work on memory or processor chips should be done only by someone who has experience in working with internal components of a computer. There are a number of precautions that need to be taken whenever the computer's cover is removed—if these precautions are not taken, serious damage to the computer can result. This book will not address in detail the steps involved in placing and removing components on the chip level; for instructions on these repairs, computer-specific manuals and guides should be consulted, and training should be obtained.

Expansion boards

If an expansion board that has been installed appears to be malfunctioning—which is often the cause when a peripheral device suddenly stops functioning properly—there are some preliminary steps that can be taken before it is returned to its manufacturer for board-level repairs or replacement.

When working on expansion boards, it is important not to touch the flat sides of the boards; this can result in damage to their very sensitive integrated circuits; instead, always hold boards by their edges. When handling boards, it can be easy to dislodge other internal components; it is critical that all operations inside the computer be done gently and precisely.

One of the most common reasons for board failure is that the board has become loose in its slot on the motherboard. This can happen if work is done inside the computer and the board is jostled, or from stress on the cable connecting to the board. To check for this possibility, disconnect the power cord, remove the computer's cover, and disconnect the cable connected to the board (visible from the back of the machine). If the board is obviously loose, it can then be pushed firmly back into its slot.

If the board is not loose, another possibility is that its contacts may have become dirty. Remove the board carefully, and turn it over; the contacts are along the bottom edge of the card, where it fits into the slot. An ordinary pencil eraser (the soft pink sort) can be used to clean these connectors; as the eraser is *gently* rubbed along these connectors, it may be possible to see a black or white film being lifted. When the edges have been cleaned, and any stray eraser residue has been carefully brushed away, the board can be replaced in the slot.

One last thing to try if the cleaning fails to restore the board to working order is putting the board into a different slot; if the connection on the motherboard was bad, a new connection might overcome that problem.

If none of these remedies work, and the board can be positively identified as the malfunctioning component, the board itself can be packaged carefully in a static-proof plastic bag (available from many computer repair shops and vendors) and sent to the manufacturer or repair facility. If the board cannot be positively identified as the culprit, the computer will need to be checked by a trained computer technician.

Keyboard

Since the keyboard is handled more than any other hardware component of a microcomputer system, it is not surprising that it is particularly susceptible to failures. Spills, dust, and the oil from fingertips all work their way down past and under the keys, making contacts sticky and shorting out connections.

If the keyboard has stopped functioning completely, or if the computer displays a "keyboard error" message on the screen, the problem may be in the cable connecting the keyboard to the computer. Verify that both connections are snug and secure. Try removing the cable, cleaning the connections on each end (the pencil eraser method works here, as well), and reattaching it.

If neither of the above methods produce results, try plugging the keyboard into another computer of the same model (if one is available). If the keyboard works, the problem is in the computer system itself, and is probably not user serviceable. If it still doesn't work, there may be a short or failure in the keyboard circuitry, and it should be checked out by an authorized repair facility.

When the failure is intermittent, it often indicates a loose or cracked circuit board—since keyboards are easily dropped, cracked circuit boards are not an unusual occurrence. When the keyboard is turned over, several small screws should be evident. Removing these screws allows the removal of the keyboard's bottom panel, exposing the internal circuitry. If the board appears to have cracks, the keyboard should be taken to a dealer for replacement. If no cracks are evident, the screws holding the board in place should be tightened, and the back panel replaced. After the keyboard has been reassembled, any available keyboard diagnostics should be run. Should the problem reappear, the keyboard should be serviced by a technician.

When the keyboard works properly except for the operation of particular keys—either the key will not generate the appropriate character when pressed, or it sticks and repeats when pressed—often the problem is simply dirt under the keypad. Key covers (the plastic piece with the character printed on it) can be removed using a flat-blade screwdriver. Place the edge of the blade under the key, and use it as a lever to pry the key cover off its post. Once the post is exposed, it can be sprayed with contact cleaner or WD-40. Replace the key cover by pressing it firmly back onto the post. If the key still does not work, the keyboard may have a more serious problem; try the steps outlined above for checking the circuit board, or take it in for servicing.

One last problem that can be encountered with a keyboard is the gradual change in the "feel" of the keys. Over time, keys that are used frequently may begin to feel "mushy" to the touch—less solid in their travel than the other keys on the keyboard. This is due to the weakening of the springs under the key. It is possible to purchase replacement springs for the keyboard, although it is important to make sure the springs are actually designed for the keyboard type being repaired, as they can vary in size and shape.

The key covers should be removed using the procedures described above. When the post has been exposed, the spring can be lifted off of it and replaced with a new one. The key cover can then be snapped back on. This should provide the keyboard with its original "springy" feel.

Display monitor

The most common problem with a display monitor is that nothing appears on the screen. There are a number of potential reasons why this can happen, and a range of solutions that can be attempted before a repair facility needs to be contacted.

One reason for a blank display may be that a screen saver program has been installed. These programs blank out the screen after a specified period of inactivity, to prevent characters from being "burnt-in" to the screen. More advanced screen saver programs usually display a randomly changing pattern on the screen to alert the user to the fact that the monitor is not broken, but only on hold. If the screen has been completely blanked by one of these programs, however, all that is usually necessary to restore the display is pressing one of the keys on the keyboard.

Another easy to solve problem involves the brightness and contrast knobs for the monitor. If these have been improperly adjusted, they can cause the display to "disappear." This type of misadjustment can also result in distorted displays, particularly when bold text is being displayed.

Like other peripherals, monitors can stop working properly because the cables have come loose from their connections, or because the video card to which they are attached has a loose or dirty connection.

When a video card is malfunctioning, other symptoms can manifest themselves. These can include a crackling or whining noise from the monitor, intermittent failures, or distortions of the display. The same techniques apply for cleaning and reseating video cards as for the expansion boards discussed in the section above.

A distorted display does not always indicate a problem with the video card, however. It can also result from improper adjustments of the monitor settings, or malfunctioning of internal components. If the monitor shipped with diagnostic tools, or if you have a diskette with a generic screen diagnostic routine, that program should be run. It will assist in identifying the type and degree of distortion, since these problems are easier to recognize using diagnostic patterns than with a standard text character display. If the display grid does appear to be symmetrical, it may be possible to adjust the appearance using "potentiometers" that are accessible from the back of the monitor. Using a tuning wand (usually included in basic microcomputer maintenance kits), turn these "pots" either clockwise or counter-clockwise to bring the screen back into proper alignment.

Other display problems that occur, including distortion or blurring of the screen, problems with the power supply, or malfunctioning video boards, will need to be dealt with by technicians trained on the specific brand of monitor.

Floppy disk drive

The mechanical parts of a floppy disk drive get a good bit of use, particularly on a public access computer; each time a diskette is inserted into the machine, written to, or removed, moving parts are utilized. Over time, these parts can become misaligned, worn down, or completely dysfunctional.

If the drive will not allow a diskette to be inserted, the problem can be as simple as an upside down diskette. All disk drives require that the diskette be inserted in the proper position. Most diskettes have labels or arrows indicating the direction in which they are to be inserted; however, when these labels have been removed or obscured, users will sometimes have problems recognizing the "right" side from the "wrong" side. There are certain physical clues on any diskette—the write-protect tabs and the "window" through which the magnetic surface is accessed are two of these clues—which allow the user to identify the top and bottom of the diskette. By comparing the diskette without proper labelling to a newer diskette or program diskette with clear insertion directions, the problem can usually be resolved.

If the diskette is being held properly, but the drive still will not allow it to be inserted, do *not* attempt to force the diskette into the drive. This will probably damage the diskette, and can quite possibly cause further damage to the drive. The drive should be examined by a technician.

If a diskette has been placed in drive, and the computer has difficulty in reading it, several possibilities can be explored. First, the diskette may not have been formatted before it was inserted. All computers require that diskettes be formatted properly for their operating system. On a Macintosh system, the computer will offer to format the diskette upon insertion; on an IBM compatible system, only an error message will be displayed.

When the disk can be read, but data cannot be written to it, the write-protect tabs may have been enabled. On a 5-1/4" diskette, this involves placing a sticker over the notch on the top right side of the diskette; if the sticker is removed, data can once again be written to the disk. On a 3-1/2" diskette, a small plastic tab is slid from its position blocking a hole in the diskette cover to a position above the hole; to disable the write protection, the tab can be slid back down to cover the hole.

Another explanation for disk read or write errors is that the diskette being used may be the wrong density for the drive. As new models of microcomputers have been developed, a wider range of diskette types have become available. On IBM compatible computers using 5-1/4" drives, there are both low-density (360K) and high-density (1.2 megabytes) diskettes. On IBM compatible computers using 3-1/2" drives, there are also low-density (720K) and high-density (1.44 megabytes) diskettes. On Macintosh computers, which use only 3-1/2 drives, there are single-sided low-density (400K), double-sided low-density (800K), and double-sided high-density (1.44MB) diskettes.

Most disk drives are downwardly compatible, meaning that a drive that reads high-density and/or double-sided diskettes can probably read and write to low-density and/or single-sided diskettes as well. The reverse, however is not true; low-density or single-sided drives *cannot* write to high-density or double-sided diskettes. This is where drive read and write errors occur most commonly, particularly in environments with a mix of computer types.

If a low-density diskette has been formatted on an IBM compatible with a high-density drive, problems in reading and writing the diskette from a low density drive can also occur. Although in theory the high-density drive should be able to format a low-density diskette (using a FORMAT/4 command), in reality this process often does not work properly. It is always safer to format a low-density diskette on a low-density drive— the diskette can then be used safely on either a high or low-density drive.

If a diskette cannot be read or written to, and if none of the above situations appears to be applicable, the diskette itself may simply have become unusable. Magnetic media is not by nature particularly durable, and any number of factors ranging from magnetic fields to spilled coffee can render it useless. Data on a bad disk can sometimes be salvaged by copying it to a good disk, or by running a utility program like the Norton Utilities on it. Some manufacturers of diskettes (most notably 3M) will attempt to recover data from a damaged diskette if it is sent back to them. However, if the disk is badly damaged, it may not be possible to recover the data.

If the disk drive problem persists with more than one diskette, it is likely that the problem is in the drive itself rather than the diskette. The number of options available to the end-user are then reduced.

Sometimes disk read/write errors occur because the drive heads have become dirtied with residue from diskettes. It is possible to clean the drives with disk drive cleaning kits; these kits can be purchased through most computer and office supply stores. Use of these cleaning kits is discussed in Chapter 11; they should not be overused, as their abrasive action can wear down drive heads. If the drives have not been cleaned in over 6 months, and there has been regular use of the floppy drive, cleaning the drive may solve the problem.

Other floppy drive problems generally require the assistance of a trained technician, as adjustments or repairs of the drive mechanism or controller can be very difficult to do.

Hard disk drives

Hard drives of all types are often prone to failure. It is not a question of *whether* a hard drive is going to fail; it is rather a question of *when* the failure is going to occur. In fact, drives are often rated by MTBF, or "Mean Time Between Failures." If a drive is being backed up regularly, a hard disk crash will be less catastrophic (see Chapter 11). In any case, however, the loss of the use of a hard drive, even for a short time, can severely limit the usefulness of a computer.

Some hard drive problems are easy to correct. As with any peripheral device, the card and/or cable attached to the drive may have come loose. On an IBM-compatible microcomputer, the hard drive is generally connected by an internal cable to a hard disk controller card on the motherboard. This card, and the cable connecting it to the hard drive, can sometimes come loose.

If the disk can be accessed, but data cannot be read, a number of utilities are available to assist the user in recovering data and diagnosing the problem. On IBM-compatibles, the Norton Utilities, PC Tools Deluxe, and Mace Utilities are all commercial packages designed to diagnose hard drive problems and recover data from damaged or dysfunctional disks. On Macintosh computers, Symantec Utilities for the Macintosh and Mac Tools Deluxe perform a similar function. Some of these programs, if purchased before a crash, include utilities that make data recovery even easier—more information on these utilities is provided in Chapter 11.

If data recovery utilities are unable to retrieve data from the disk and report back on the cause of the problem, a reformatting of the drive can be attempted. This should include both a low-level format and a high-level format; for more information on the proper method for performing these formats, the user will need to refer to the documentation for the specific disk drive.

If reformatting does not cause the disk to be readable again, the drive (and, if applicable, the hard drive controller card) should be looked at by a trained technician.

Modem

When a modem is malfunctioning, there are few options available to the user for on-the-spot repairs. If the modem is internal (on a card that sits in one of the internal slots on the motherboard), the procedures described under "Expansion boards" may be helpful in resolving the problem. If it is an external modem, the problem may be as simple as a disconnected or loose cable. Be sure to check both cables: the one running from the modem to the computer, *and* the one from the modem to the telephone jack. The problem also may stem from a bad telephone connection; this can be checked by plugging a standard telephone into the wall jack, and checking for a dial tone.

When communications sessions are interrupted by strings of garbled characters (also known as "line noise"), there are a number of possible explanations. If there is a telephone handset on the same line as the modem, picking up the handset can (and probably will) result in line noise being generated. Similarly, features such as call waiting, which send an audible tone over the line, can disrupt or even disconnect a telecommunications link. Line noise can also result from problems in the telephone connections between certain telephone switching stations. If line noise is a continuing problem when calling some locations but not others, the telephone company should be notified so that appropriate repairs can be made.

Other problems with the modem should be referred to a technician or to the manufacturer, since the internal components of a modem are not user-serviceable.

Printer

If a printer is not printing at all, there are a few basic steps that should be taken. First, of course, all cable connections should be checked to be sure that they are not loose or detached. This includes both the cable that connects the printer to the power supply, and the cable that connects the printer to the computer. When checking the cable to the computer, note which type of port the cable is connected to: on an IBM, it will be either parallel or serial (9 or 25-pin), on a Macintosh it can be a square 9-pin or round 8-pin connector, and can be attached at either the printer port or the modem port. This information will be necessary in other trouble-shooting steps if the cable connections are not at fault.

The next thing to check is whether the printer is "online" or whether it is "offline" or "local." These mean, respectively, able to receive instructions from the computer, or receiving instructions only from the controls on the printer itself. Generally, a printer is kept online most of the time, and is changed to offline or local mode when paper needs to be advanced or changed, or adjustments need to be made to the print quality or type. If the printer is taken offline, it will not be able to accept instructions from the computer, and may therefore appear to be malfunctioning. Turning it online will allow it to print again.

Some software programs require that a "printer driver" be installed in order for the program to print properly. These drivers are generally shipped with the software program, or can be ordered from the publisher of the program. Printer drivers contain instructions that let the program format data properly for a given printer; if the program does not find the proper driver, it may refuse to print, or may print "garbage" characters on the page. Contact the software publisher for information on available printer drivers.

It may also be necessary to tell the computer's system software which communication port the printer is attached to. Computers using the MS-DOS operating system can use the MODE command for this purpose. This command uses the designations LPT1, LPT2, COM1, and COM2 to refer to the first and second parallel ports and first and second serial ports, respectively. (If additional communication ports are installed in the computer, they can be designated as LPT3 or COM3, etc., as needed.) DOS assumes that printer output should be sent to LPT1 (the first parallel port) unless the software specifies otherwise. It is possible to change this default using the MODE command. The DOS manual will provide more detailed information on how this redirection is accomplished. The command can then be placed in the AUTOEXEC.BAT file, so it will be executed each time the computer is turned on. When a printer will not print at all, it is often because the MODE command is not set properly.

On the Macintosh, printer and port selection are done through the Chooser desk accessory. All printer drivers available are shown in the Chooser window, and once a printer has been selected, the choice of printer or modem port can be defined. If the proper driver or port has not been selected in the Chooser window, the printer will not respond when a print command is chosen.

If the printer is working, but the print quality is poor, there are a multitude of potential reasons for the problem. Before any of these possibilities are explored, a self-test of the printer should be run. On most printers, this involves holding down some combination of setting buttons while turning the printer on; for the specific routine required, the manual should be consulted. If the self-test shows good quality printed output, the problem may well be based in the printer driver for the software, and the publisher of the application package should be contacted. If the self-test shows the same problems in print quality, the problem is probably mechanical and the procedures below can be used for identifying the underlying cause.

On a dot-matrix or daisy-wheel printer, poor print quality can often be traced to the ribbon. It can become jammed, or dried out from long use. If the problem is that the ribbon is not advancing, it may be possible to advance it by hand until the jammed portion has been threaded through the cartridge. If the problem is intermittent poor quality, there may be a dry spot on the ribbon that passes through on a regular basis. It is often easiest just to replace the cartridge with a new one.

If the printer has a forms adjustment that allows it to accommodate multi-part forms more easily, an improper setting of this adjustment can affect print quality. The option for thicker paper or forms moves the print head further from the page; if standard paper is used while the print head is in this position, poor print quality can result.

Over time, the print head can become coated with dust and/or ink. The print head can be cleaned, using a cleaner or solvent applied to a cotton swab. Often, cleaning the print head, along with other portions of the printer, will result in greatly improved output.

145

On a laser printer, the print quality will deteriorate when the printer begins running low on toner. Most printers will signal when more toner is required, and will give sufficient warning to the user before print quality deteriorates. If the printer is used heavily, it is a good idea to keep spare toner cartridges available for immediate replacement. At times the toner can shift to one side of the cartridge, it can also affect the quality. If the print is uneven in its density, taking the toner cartridge out, shaking it, and replacing it in the printer can often solve the problem.

Many laser printers need to be cleaned on a regular basis. In the case of several types of laser printer, the documentation explaining the cleaning routine is difficult to read and/or incomplete. For example, the HP LaserJet Series II needs to have several internal wires cleaned regularly, but the documentation does not clearly indicate the location of all of these wires. If the printer is exhibiting poor print quality even after cleaning and replacement of the toner cartridge, the manufacturer should be contacted directly, so that any additional information on cleaning or user-serviceable parts can be obtained.

If these procedures fail to improve the quality of output from the printer, it will be necessary to have the printer serviced by a repair facility. With printers, it is especially important to look for a facility that has been authorized by the manufacturer to work on that brand of equipment. Without this authorization, repair shops can have difficulty in obtaining parts for the printers.

Disks and stored data files

The issues of data recovery were touched upon in Chapter 11, in the discussion of preventive maintenance for disks and stored data files. Responsive maintenance for magnetically stored files can be much easier and more reliable when disk utility programs have been installed before the file was lost. In addition, a regular backup routine ensures that lost files can be replaced with a recent version if the file itself cannot be recovered.

The sections below address methods for recovering files once they have been lost or damaged. The first section covers the basic process of file recovery, in cases where files have been accidentally deleted or damaged. The second section addresses the issues of viruses and data loss or damage resulting from harmful computer programs.

File recovery

Most computer users, no matter how careful, eventually find themselves deleting a file they wish they'd kept, or erasing a directory full of necessary information. In fact, although most operating systems provide some sort of warning before a global deletion takes place, people who use a computer frequently have a tendency to ignore these warning messages and jump right to the deletion. When the file (or files) are critical, file recovery software is essential.

There are a number of utilities available for microcomputers that will "undelete" files that have been erased from the disk. The reason this feat can be accomplished is that when the computer receives a command to erase or delete a file, all it really does is remove the information on that file from the disk's table of contents (called the FAT, or file allocation table). The portions of the disk on which the file resides are not actually erased, but they are made available to other files that are saved later on. This makes it important to run file recovery programs *before* any new data is saved to the disk, since new data may be written over the parts of the disk where the mistakenly deleted file is stored.

On IBM-compatible computers, the Norton Utilities was the first package to provide user-friendly file recovery capability. It has since been joined by programs such as PC Tools Deluxe and the Mace Utilities, among others. On the Macintosh, Symantec Utilities for the Macintosh and Mac Tools Deluxe provide similar features. Each of these programs has its own strengths and weaknesses; if the library's budget will allow it, having copies of a number of disk utility programs can be an excellent safety measure.

If files have been lost through a hard drive crash or a malicious computer virus, the same utilities can be pressed into service. With many of these utility packages, programs are provided that can be installed before the disk crashes or files are lost. This can greatly improve the likelihood of disk or file restoration if a major catastrophe occurs.

Virus detection and eradication

As viruses proliferate in the microcomputer world, it becomes more difficult to point to specific symptoms that will allow users to identify their presence. One of the best methods for staying aware of new potential threats to microcomputer safety is through users groups and electronic bulletin boards. Not only will members of these groups often know of new viruses and their symptoms, but they will also be aware of the most recent versions of virus detection and eradication programs.

Currently, there are some commercial and shareware packages that will assist users in detecting viruses that might be present on their disks and removing the harmful programs without damaging legitimate data. Some of these programs are mentioned in Chapter 11, since they include preventive as well as responsive measures. However, the constant evolution of virus programs makes it impossible to provide a comprehensive list of virus detection programs here. The user group and BBS route is most likely to yield up-to-date and useful information.

Chapter 13

Maintenance Costs

Maintenance of microcomputers carries with it a number of costs, ranging from the salaries of in-house technicians and the purchase of appropriate tools to the expense of a full-scale outside maintenance contract. These costs are inescapable, since all microcomputer equipment will eventually be in need of repair or upgrade services. Every library manager needs to make his or her own decision, based on available institutional and financial resources, as to what combination of options should be implemented for maintenance of the library's microcomputer equipment.

In this chapter, the costs associated with the many options for microcomputer repair are outlined, and the pros and cons of maintenance contracts and in-house repair facilities are considered. There are no "right" or "wrong" ways to handle maintenance of library microcomputers; the costs and benefits of each option need to be weighed in light of the library's needs and resources.

In-house maintenance

Libraries that are part of larger organizations—e.g., a university or a corporation—will often have access to internal repair facilities with trained technicians. When such facilities are available, they will often be the most cost-effective solution. They will not, however, be without cost. Most organizations offering in-house support services do charge for their services. In some cases, there is a direct fee for equipment repairs and/or purchase of parts. In others, the overall costs of the repairs done by the facility, including such overhead costs as salaries and supplies, are charged back to departments based on the total number of computers and peripherals owned by that department.

In organizations where a charge-back method is used, it is important for managers to determine the approximate charge-back costs per machine *before* purchases of equipment are made. These fixed maintenance costs will need to be taken into account in the initial budgeting for the computers. Although the additional expense can appear as an unfair charge for a library with new equipment that has a good repair track record, the advantage to this type of charge-back is that the library will not be surprised by large repair bills as the equipment ages. Like an insurance policy, this type of maintenance charge allows for more accurate budgeting.

Libraries with a large number of installed microcomputers and peripherals, but no established in-house repair facility, may wish to consider hiring a trained microcomputer technician on a full- or part-time basis. Having an in-house technician available can greatly reduce the costs incurred at outside repair centers. Even in cases where the library's technician cannot repair the problem, the preliminary diagnostic work done will result in a lower charge from the outside facility; often, much of the hourly charge at an outside facility will consist of the time spent determining the nature of the problem.

Even those libraries with in-house microcomputer technicians will at times need to turn to an outside repair facility. This can happen for several reasons:

- •First, if the warranty period has not ended, the vendor or another authorized representative of the equipment manufacturer should do the repair work and replace parts as necessary so as not to void the warranty;

- •Second, some equipment manufacturers will only provide replacement parts to authorized repair facilities; and

•Third, with equipment such as laser printers or CD-ROM drives, it is not cost-effective to maintain the expensive equipment necessary to do internal repairs.

It is in the library's best interest to identify available repair facilities *before* the immediate need for one arises. This allows careful evaluation of local facilities, and helps prevent problems when repairs do need to be sent out. The section below provides some criteria to be used in this evaluation process.

Evaluating repair facilities

The repair business is very competitive, and rates can vary substantially from one vendor to another. The quality of service provided by computer repair shops can vary as well, and *not* always in relation to their prices. For these reasons, it is important to perform a careful evaluation of repair options before sending a piece of equipment out for maintenance, and most certainly before signing a contract for regular maintenance work.

There are a number of methods for gathering names of local repair facilities. One of the first places to check is with the vendor (or vendors) from which the equipment was purchased. If the vendor does not service the equipment, it should be able to provide the name of at least one facility that is authorized to do repairs on the brand of equipment purchased.

The next place to check is with any internal computing organization, such as a data processing department in a company or a university computing center. If they do not provide in-house service as described in the section above, they will have information on available repair services that have been approved for use by institutional computer users.

Another valuable resource for recommendations is the list of libraries and other users that was compiled in the original computer planning process (see Chapter 2). If users groups or electronic bulletin board systems in the area have been identified, these too can yield helpful information on both reliable and unreliable microcomputer service centers.

Once a list has been compiled, each facility should be evaluated on the basis of the following criteria:

• References from customers, with particular attention to satisfaction with quality and efficiency of work;

• Brands of equipment for which they provide manufacturer-authorized service (including access to parts from the manufacturer);

• Cost per hour of labor, as well as pricing for parts (one way to evaluate the pricing of parts is to ask for replacement cost estimates on one or two commonly serviced parts, such as a 40-megabyte hard drive or VGA video card);

• Length of time the facility has been in business;

• Ratio of technicians to customers, and technicians to covered machines (particularly important if an on-site contract is being considered);

• If an on-site service contract is being considered, the response time guaranteed after a problem is reported (if the time is given in hours, be sure to find out whether those refer to *working* hours, and if so, what those working hours are); and

• Whether or not loaner equipment will be provided if an on-site technician determines that repair will need to be done in the shop.

Based on this information, it should be possible to make an informed and effective decision as to which repair facility to utilize.

If the library is using an outside vendor only for occasional maintenance tasks, the choice of which facility to use is less critical. If one vendor provides unacceptable service, it is easy to utilize another on the next call. Those libraries with a large number of microcomputer systems, and without in-house maintenance support, will often be interested in setting up a contractual relationship with a single vendor. In these cases, the evaluation of available facilities is particularly important, since it is often difficult to break the terms of a service contract.

Service contracts

In her book on the Apple II computer as a library public access machine, Jean Armour Polly had this to say about maintenance contracts:

> The chances that something will fail within the warranty period are remote, but the chances that something major will fail after that period is over are even more remote. Librarians would be better served to spend some money on computer cleaning supplies and plan a preventative maintenance program than to gamble on the wrong side of the odds, paying the dealer for service they will never need.[13]

Although this optimism was warranted in the earlier days of library automation, as microcomputers have become more complex and diverse, the justification for maintenance contracts has grown. The increased use of such technically sophisticated peripherals as hard disks, CD-ROM drives, laser printers and high-speed modems, has led to similarly increased rates of failure; this in turn results in greater requirements for maintenance.

Another advantage of a standing maintenance contract is faster response. Without a contract, a library must arrange for a malfunctioning piece of equipment to be transported to the service facility. It is then not unusual for repairs to take a week or more, following which the component must be either picked up by a library staff member or shipped back to the library through a parcel service. If the library depends on the computer in question for daily tasks, the loss of the machine for weeks at a time can be crippling. With an on-site service contract, the higher charges bring with them added convenience.

Libraries choosing to invest in a regular maintenance contract generally have two options available. The first is a comprehensive

---

[13]Polly, Jean Armour. *Essential Guide to Apple Computers in Libraries: Volume 1, Public Technology: the Library Public Access Computer.* Westport, CT: Meckler, 1986. p.18.

maintenance contract, which acts as a full insurance policy against any failure of the computers. The second is a time and materials contract, which generally lowers the hourly labor rate and parts replacement charges incurred by the customer. The sections below address the advantages and disadvantages of these two types of contracts.

Comprehensive maintenance contracts

Most repair facilities offer their clients the option of a full maintenance contract. In such a contract, the user pays a flat fee for each piece of equipment that will be covered, including system units *and* peripherals. The price per item will vary based on the cost of the unit, the difficulty of repair, and the failure rate that the facility has experienced with that type of equipment. Thus, a 386 microcomputer with a VGA monitor, a large hard drive, and an attached laser printer is likely to have a much higher annual maintenance charge than an 8088-based PC with a monochrome monitor, two floppy disk drives, and a dot-matrix printer.

For the monthly or annual charge, the components are covered for all necessary repairs. When a computer or peripheral fails, the repair service is contacted, and a technician is dispatched within a pre-arranged length of time (generally ranging from two to eight working hours). In many cases, the contract also specifies that a piece of comparable equipment will be provided on loan if the repairs cannot be performed on-site by the technician.

The biggest disadvantage of a comprehensive maintenance contract is generally its cost. The annual cost to cover a large microcomputer installation can be considerable, and it represents a substantial investment on the part of the library. If the funding is available, however, this type of contract provides the greatest piece of mind for the facility manager, and the least amount of downtime for the computer users.

Time and materials contracts

Libraries that need the convenience of an on-site service contract, but are unable to afford the high prices of a comprehensive maintenance contract, should consider the option of a time and materials service contract. In a time and materials contract, the library still pays an hourly labor charge, and is charged for any replacement parts that are installed when a component fails. Generally, the hourly charge is reduced from the amount a non-contractual customer would pay, and the parts cost is also slightly lower.

The real advantage of a time and materials contract, however, is that it gives the library the advantage of on-site service if needed, thereby reducing the amount of time involved in having repairs done. In many cases, loaner equipment can also be negotiated as part of a time and materials contract.

Many repair facilities do charge a per-unit fee for each computer or peripheral device that will be covered under the time and materials contract. This fee is generally substantially lower than the charge for a full maintenance contract. There are also repair vendors that will provide blanket time and materials contracts without imposing a per-unit charge; these vendors will generally ask for a contractual commitment to use only that repair shop, or will set up a deposit account, to ensure that the contract is a profitable one for them even without the annual charges. With time and materials contracts, it is particularly important to shop around for good deals.

Appendix A

Glossary

A

Acoustic coupler: Data communications device into which a telephone handset can be placed, allowing a computer to communicate to another device via telephone lines, typically at lower speeds (300 bps or less).

Alpha-numeric: Describes data that consists of the upper and lower case letters of the alphabet, and the numerals zero through nine.

American National Standards Institute (ANSI): An organization responsible for setting technical standards within the United States.

Analog: A method of data transmission in which the signals change smoothly, in an unbroken stream; this term can also be used to designate computer components using this mode of transmission. See also Digital.

ARCNET: A networking protocol and set of products developed by the Datapoint Corporation.

Artificial intelligence: A goal of computer programming in which computers would emulate human logic in the analysis of problems.

ASCII: The commonly used abbreviation for American Standard Code for Information Interchange. This character set uses 7 bits of binary information to represent letters, numbers, symbols and various control functions to exchange information between different computer systems.

Assembler language: A programming language consisting of symbolic machine language statements which have a one-to-one correspondence with the microprocessor's internal instruction set. Programs written in assembler language execute more quickly than those written in higher-level languages, which lack this one-to-one correspondence.

Asynchronous communication: A widely used communication method that does not require an exact timing relationship between the two ends of the connection. Each system signals the start and end of each character it sends to the other system. See also Communications protocol.

Auto-answer: The ability of a modem or other data communications device to establish a connection to an incoming data call without user intervention.

Autodial: The ability of a modem or other data communications device to place an outgoing data call without user intervention.

B

Background processing: Low priority computer processing tasks which take place while another processing application or activity is displayed to the user. See also Foreground processing.

Backup: The process by which copies of computer files are stored in a secondary location as protection against data loss following computer failures.

Backup copy: A copy of stored computer data and programs, used to restore information when the original data is corrupted or destroyed.

Bar-code scanner: A device used to read bar-code labels (such as UPC codes or book labels) by means of reflected light.

BASIC (Beginner's All-purpose Symbolic Instruction Code): A widely used high-level programming language, available for use on most microcomputer systems.

Batch: A processing method in which a group of programs or complex instruction sequences are collected and then processed in one complete sequence. See also Transaction processing.

Baud: Often confused with bits-per-second, baud means the number of modem signals transmitted per second on a communication link. With high speed modems, these signals typically carry more than one binary bit.

BBS: Bulletin Board System. See Electronic bulletin board.

Benchmark: A standard point of reference against which computer hardware or software performance can be measured. Benchmark tests are often used in comparative reviews of equipment and/or programs.

Bernoulli Box: A data storage unit for microcomputers which provides removable hard disk storage cartridges, allowing the convenience of multiple floppy disks with the high storage capacity of hard disks.

Beta test: The stage in the software product development cycle where the program is distributed for testing in actual use situations.

Bibliographic database: A collection of bibliographic citations stored in a computerized database, allowing complex searching, sorting, and formatting of the citations.

Bidrectional printing: A printer feature of dot-matrix and daisy-wheel printers that allows output when the print head is moving either left to right or right to left. This feature results in faster printing.

Binary code: The base 2 number system used by computer systems, in which information is represented by combinations of "0s" and "1s."

Bit: The basic unit of information in digital computer processing, representing 0 or 1; also known as a binary digit. See also Byte.

Bit-mapped: Screen display which corresponds exactly to a binary matrix (bitmap) stored in the computer's memory.

Block: A group of characters or bytes in a single related unit; often used to represent segments of memory or disk storage space.

Board: See Circuit board.

Bomb: See Crash.

Booting: The process by which a computer loads initial instructions into memory upon startup; comes from "bootstrap program," which originally referred to the phrase "pulling itself up by its bootstraps." See also Cold boot, Warm boot, and Rebooting.

BPS: Bits per second; the speed of binary data which is transmitted over a communications link. See also Baud and Modem.

Buffer: A storage area used by a computer when the destination for the data is unable to process the blocks of information quickly enough; often used between a processor and a printer, or a keyboard and a processor.

Bug: An error or defect in a software program; originates from early computer usage when insects would often become lodged in vital components, causing unexpected failures.

Bundling: A computer marketing strategy in which additional items such as software and accessories are included in the purchase price of hardware components.

Bus: A path for the transmission of electronic data within a computer system; generally used in the description of specific microcomputer architectures, e.g., "AT bus" to refer to the method for information interchange within an IBM-AT type computer.

Byte: A unit of data consisting of eight consecutive binary bits of information. Most computer systems measure memory and disk storage capacity in bytes.

C

Cache memory: An area of computer memory which holds the most recently used program instructions or data, based on the principle that many of these are likely to be used again; use of cache memory can significantly increase the speed of program execution.

CAI: Computer aided instruction; software programs that are used in training applications, as supplements to or replacements for more conventional training methods.

CD-ROM : Compact disc-read-only memory. A type of optical disk commonly used for storage of machine-readable data and programs; also used for the storage and replaying of audio signals. See also Optical storage.

Central processing unit (CPU): The collection of electronic circuitry responsible for the execution of all program instructions and manipulation of data within a computer system. In microcomputers, the CPU is typically contained in a single very-large-scale integrated circuit.

Centronics interface: A type of parallel communications interface that is used for printer connections to microcomputers such as the IBM PC.

Character recognition: See Optical character recognition.

Chips: See Integrated Circuit.

Circuit: An electrical transmission path providing communication between two points.

Circuit board: A board made of insulating material with printed wiring connections for integrated circuit chips and other electronic components.

Clock: A timing device which generates regular signal pulses to synchronize the various internal operations of a computer system; a higher clock speed increases a computer's instruction processing speed.

Clock speed: The rate at which a computer clock generates pulses; usually measured in megahertz, or millions of pulses per second.

CMOS (Complimentary Metal Oxide Semiconductor): A type of integrated circuit technology which consumes little power, has high immunity to noise, and can operate with a relatively unregulated power source; often used in devices such as laptop or portable computers, in which power usage is a key factor.

Coaxial cable: Cabling used in many high speed data communications applications, and in mainframe terminal to host connections; consists of a single insulated center conductor, usually copper wire, completely surrounded by a concentric shield of braided wire or conducting foil.

Cold boot: Complete re-initialization of a computer system, usually from a powered-down state. See also Booting, Rebooting, and Warm boot.

Command-driven: A user interface that requires the user to type commands in the proper syntax in order to control a program or operate a computer; compare with Menu-driven.

Communications protocol: The standards used by one computer system to communicate with another. Since a number of protocols are commonly used, the same protocol must be specified at each end in order for communication to take place. Simple asynchronous communication protocols require the definition of bit rate (bps), data word length, parity, and start and stop bits. Other protocols provide the ability to regulate the flow of data and correct communication errors.

Compatibility: The degree to which data and application programs from different computer systems can be used interchangeably.

Computer network: The interconnection of two or more computers, allowing the sharing of data and/or peripherals; see also Local area network.

Connect time: The period of time during which a user is connected via data communication equipment to a remote computer such as an online database host or bulletin board service.

Contention: Competition for system resources between two or more computer devices attempting simultaneous access.

Co-processor: A specialized computer chip which can be added to a microcomputer's main logic board to speed the completion of tasks; most often used to accelerate complex graphic or mathematical operations.

Crash: Unexpected computer program or processor failure which can result in lost or corrupted data. See also Head crash.

CRT (cathode ray tube): A vacuum tube device used as a display screen; generally used to refer to any video terminal device.

Cut and paste: An editing operation that allows the user to move text and/or graphic information from one location or document to another.

Cut-sheet feeder: A device that allows a dot-matrix or daisy-wheel printer to use separate sheets of paper, rather than pin-fed computer paper.

D

Daisy-chain: A method of connecting computers or other devices on a network in a serial manner, wherein the data passes through each unit on its way to the next.

Daisy-wheel printer: A printer utilizing a metal or plastic print wheel to imprint high-quality character images onto a page in a manner similar to many typewriter mechanisms.

Database: A computer file of individual information records that share a pre-defined format.

Database management system (DBMS): An application program that provides the capacity to store and update information in a database, and to retrieve, sort, and/or report that information based on user-defined criteria.

Data communications: The transmission and reception of computer-based information.

Data compression: The process of reducing the size of a computer data file for more efficient storage or transmission, by removing unnecessary gaps and redundant information in the file.

Data conversion: The process of converting data files created for one program or computer system into a form that can be read by another system.

DBF: A file format used by Ashton-Tate's popular dBase database program.

DBMS: See Database management system.

Dedicated line: A communications line used for a single data communications purpose, such as microcomputer modem communications or facsimile machine use.

Default: The initial value assumed by a computer program for data which can be entered by the user; also, the pre-set choice from among several options presented to the user. If the user does not enter any data or does not make a specific choice, the program uses the default value.

Desktop publishing: The process of page layout composition, design, and production using microcomputer-based software programs.

DIF (Data Interchange Format): A file format used for the interchange of spreadsheet files among varying spreadsheet application programs.

Digital: Coding of data in which the information is represented by a sequence of discrete elements; in computers, this often refers to electrical on/off impulses used to represent the binary digits 1 and 0. See also Analog.

Digitize: To convert an image or audio signal into digital format.

DIP switch: A Dual In-line Package switch; a small, multi-position switch found on some microcomputer circuit boards which is used to reconfigure certain aspects of the equipment's processing functions.

Disk: See Magnetic media; Disk drive.

Disk drive: A peripheral device that uses magnetic media in the form of diskettes to hold information; can be used to refer to a drive reading floppy diskettes or a hard disk drive.

Disk operating system: See Operating system.

Disk sector: A segment of a track on a magnetic disk. See also Disk track.

Disk track: A circular segment of a magnetic disk upon which data is stored; broadly analogous to the tracks on magnetic recording tape.

Diskette: A flexible disk coated with magnetic material and used for storing information. See also Magnetic media.

Display: The representation in visual form of data from a computer system; can refer to monitors or paper printouts.

Distributed processing: The use of multiple interconnected computer systems to perform a related set of of data storage and processing tasks.

Document: A collection of information that can be read by a person or by a computer program; this can refer to a printed report or to a data file created on a computer.

Documentation: The information which accompanies computer hardware and software that explains its use. Documentation can be provided in printed form, or on magnetic disk, in a form readable using word processors or other specialized programs.

DOS: See Operating system.

Dot-matrix printer: A printer that forms graphics and text characters from a matrix of horizontal and vertical dot positions. Daisy wheel printers generally offer higher text quality, but they are slower and cannot print bitmap graphics.

Double density diskettes: Diskettes which allow for the storing of more information by doubling the number of tracks per inch, the density of bits serially recorded in each track, or a combination of both.

Double sided diskettes: Diskettes which allow for the storage of information on both sides of the disk.

Down time: The time during which a computer system is not operating, or otherwise unavailable to users.

Download: The process of receiving a data file or program file from another computer over a data communications link. It typically involves the use of an error-correcting protocol to ensure file integrity. See Upload.

Dumb terminal: A keyboard and video display device which is used to receive information from and send information to a host computer system, but which does not process any information itself.

Dynamic RAM: Random access memory that must constantly be refreshed with an electrical current to retain information. See also Random access memory.

E

Editor: An application program that allows the user to modify text in a program source file or text document.

Electronic bulletin board: A computer system that is designed to store files and messages; users call the system over telecommunications lines to upload or download files, and to leave messages to other users.

Electronic mail: The exchange of messages and files between users on different computer systems over communications networks using addressing and delivery conventions similar to regular mail service.

Electronic publishing: The use of computer systems to create textual and/or graphic materials ranging from printed documents to CD-ROM databases.

Electrostatic printer: A non-impact printer that utilizes electrically charged dots to attract ink, which is then embedded onto the paper by heat and pressure.

Emulation: Imitation of one computer system's operations, in whole or part, by another type of computer system.

Encryption: The conversion of data files into a form that cannot be read without converting the files back to normal format, to ensure privacy.

End-of-file marker: A symbol on magnetic media that the computer places to designate the endpoint of a given data file.

Enter key: The key on a terminal or computer keyboard that the user presses to transmit data from the display to the host processor when a command line or programming statement is complete.

Escape character: In the ASCII character set, the escape character is intended to flag subsequent characters for special interpretation by the computer. When using microcomputer software, the escape key can often be pressed to cancel or exit the current activity.

Ethernet: A high speed data transmission method widely used in local area networks.

Execute: To carry out a set of instructions or system commands.

Expansion board: A circuit board which can be inserted into a computer to increase its capabilities.

F

Facsimile: A method for transmitting images over communications lines, using a scanning procedure that encodes the image on the transmitting end and converts it into a replica of the original image on the receiving end.

Fault tolerance: The ability of a computer or program to operate without errors even in the case of hardware failures.

Fax: See Facsimile.

Fiber optics: A method of carrying data in the form of light pulses through hair-thin strands of glass. Fiber optics are totally immune to electrical interference, and can communicate information virtually error-free at speeds of several billion bits-per-second.

Field: One element of a database record. A field serves the same function, although it may hold different data entries, in all other records of a given data set.

File: A collection of related information records or text characters treated as a single unit in computer memory or on disk.

File protection: A method for preventing data on storage media from being erased or altered.

File server: A computer in a local area network that is dedicated to providing storage and processing functions for users on the network.

Fixed disk: See Hard disk.

Floppy disk: See Diskette.

Flowchart: A diagram, used as a systems analysis tool, that uses standard symbols to show the sequence of operations and the decision branching to be executed by a computer program.

Font: A character set designed with a unique type style.

Footer: Information inserted at the bottom of every page in a document, such as page numbers or titles. See also Header.

Footprint: The amount of space that a piece of equipment occupies on a desktop.

Foreground processing: High-priority processing that takes precedence over other processing tasks in a multi-tasking environment, such as servicing a user's interaction with the keyboard and screen. See also Background processing.

Form feed: The advance of tractor feed paper in a printer to the beginning of a new page.

Format: The process of writing basic data structures on the surface of a magnetic disk to permit subsequent storage of programs and data. This typically destroys any data already on a disk; also refers to the specific arrangement or layout of data in a program or database.

Fragmentation: The condition that exists when data and program files are stored in noncontiguous locations on a magnetic disk.

Friction feed: A method for advancing paper in a printer that employs rollers to grasp and move the paper, rather than using pin-feed tractors.

Full-text database: A database that contains the full record of textual material such as articles or specifications.

Function keys: Designated keys on a keyboard which do not produce characters, but which can be recognized by certain software programs to execute specific commands.

G

Gigabyte: One billion bytes.

Global search and replace: The ability of an application program to find every occurrence of a string of characters and replace it with another string.

Graphics: The display of lines and images on a computer screen or printout through the use of applications software and compatible hardware components.

H

Handshaking: The process by which two computer devices verify that a communications link has been properly established. See also Protocol.

Hard copy: Computer output in a printed form.

Hard disk: A high-capacity magnetic storage medium; can take the form of a removable cartridge or as a non-removable component of a computer.

Hardware: The physical equipment making up a computer system, including the computer system unit, monitor, keyboard, and any peripheral equipment. Contrast with Software.

Hardwired: A direct and usually inflexible link between two computer system components; often used to describe dedicated direct communications links.

Head: The component of a device that reads, writes, or erases data from a specific medium; e.g., the magnetic head of a disk drive, or the print head of a dot-matrix printer.

Head crash: The collision of the magnetic read/write head of a disk drive with the surface of a magnetic disk; often results in the destruction or corruption of data recorded on the disk.

Header: Information inserted at the top of every page in a document, such as page numbers or titles. See also Footer.

Host computer: The primary and/or controlling computer in a network consisting of multiple computers; often used to refer to large mainframe computers accessed by dumb terminals.

I

Impact printer: A printer which forms characters on paper (or other media) by physically striking a ribbon that is positioned above the paper.

Ink-jet printer: A non-impact printer which shoots a stream of electrostatically charged ink-drops at a page to form a character.

Input device: A device that collects data and converts it into a digital electronic data for use by a computer.

Input/output: Used to describe peripheral computer equipment which is used either to gather data and convert it to electronic format for processing by a computer, or to translate information from electronic format in the computer to an output such as a display or printed page; also known as I/O.

Integrated circuit: Self-contained microelectronic circuits etched on a tiny sliver of silicon substrate, and encased in a small plastic or ceramic housing with electrical contacts for mounting on circuit boards.

Integrated software: A software program which incorporates multiple application functions (e.g., spreadsheet, graphics, and database management) into a single package.

Intelligent terminal: A keyboard and video display device which is used to receive information from and send information to a host computer system, and which also processes some information itself on a local level.

Interactive: Used to describe an application which requires responses from the user as it executes; a prompted data entry system, or an airline reservations system would be examples of interactive programs.

Interface: The point of interconnection between two systems, such as a computer and a peripheral device. Some common microcomputer interfaces are parallel printer and serial (also known as RS-232) communications interfaces.

I/O: See Input/output.

J

Joystick: A device incorporating a movable lever (and sometimes one or more depressable buttons) that is used to move the position of a cursor or other marker on a display screen; often used in recreational programs.

Justification: The alignment of printed or displayed text characters along a fixed border, often the left and/or right margin of a page.

K

K: Used to represent the number 2^{10} (equal to 1,024).

Kilobyte (KB): 2^{10} bytes, or 1,024 bytes, of information; a unit of measure often used in describing disk or memory capacity and the size of machine-readable program and data files.

L

LAN: See Local area network.

Laser: A very narrow and highly focused beam of coherent electromagnetic energy in the visible light spectrum; can be used to record and/or read data from optical media.

Laser disc: See Optical storage.

LCD display: A display using liquid crystal technology; often used in laptop computers, with features such as "super-twisting" and backlighting which enhance readability.

LED display: A display using light-emitting diode technology.

Letter-quality printer: A printer that produces output suitable for high-quality correspondence, with quality comparable to or better than that produced by a standard typewriter.

Light-pen: A pen-shaped device which allows a computer operator to provide direct input to a computer by touching the display with the light-sensitive tip of the pen.

Line printer: A printer that produces an entire line of characters at one time, providing very high-speed output; often used with mini- or mainframe computers.

Local area network (LAN): A system which links together microcomputers and peripherals, allowing simultaneous or concurrent use of equipment, programs, and data among users.

M

Machine-independent: Used to describe programs which have been written in a high-level language so as to execute without depending on any unique characteristics of the different computer systems on which they might run.

Macro: A series of computer instructions referenced by a single name; by typing the macro name, the entire series of instructions is executed.

Magnetic media: Disks or tapes which are coated with magnetic material so as to allow storage of digital information.

Mass storage devices: Disk or tape drives capable of storing very large quantities of information.

Mean time between failure (MTBF): The average amount of time that a piece of equipment is likely to work before a failure occurs.

Megabyte (MB): 1,048,576 bytes (1,024K squared); often used to mean approximately one million.

Memory: The component of a computer system which holds programs and data for use by the central processing unit while the computer is active.

Menu-driven: A program which allows the user to choose commands directly from a list provided on the screen; compare with Command-driven.

MNP: Microcom Networking Protocol; an advanced form of error-checking protocol used by some modems to ensure accurate transmission of data.

Modem: From *mo*dulator-*dem*odulator; a device attached to a computer system that converts serial data in the form of binary bits into analog signals, allowing communication with other computers over telephone lines. See also Baud and BPS.

Motherboard: The central card of a computer; it generally holds the CPU and provides connections for expansion boards.

Mouse: A pointing device used on graphically oriented computer systems which moves an on-screen cursor in response to movement of the device on the desktop.

MS-DOS: Microsoft Disk Operating System. See Operating system.

Multi-processing: Used to describe a computer system that is capable of performing multiple simultaneous tasks.

Multi-tasking: The simultaneous execution of multiple tasks by a single processor.

Multi-user: A computer system that can support simultaneous access from multiple workstations.

N

Natural-language interface: A feature of some computer programing languages and operating systems that allows the user to type commands in standard English syntax.

Network topology: The arrangement of computer equipment and links in a network; can refer to this physical and/or the logical arrangement of software interactions. See also Topology.

Networking: See Local area network.

Node: Any microcomputer or terminal in a network.

Non-volatile RAM: Random access memory which retains its contents even when the computer is without power.

O

OCR: See Optical character recognition.

OEM: Original equipment manufacturer.

Office automation (OA): A general term used to refer to the range of information processing activities and equipment used in offices, including not only microcomputer use but also facsimile transmission and photocopying.

Off-the-shelf: Computer software and/or hardware that can be purchased and used with little or no adaptation to a particular environment.

Online: Used to describe terminals, microcomputers, and/or peripheral equipment which interact directly with a remote host computer system.

Operating system: The collection of programs and data that give the central processing unit its ability to manage the various internal components of the computer system, such as memory, disk drives, keyboard, and display; some examples of common microcomputer operating systems are CP/M, which was used on many early microcomputers, MS-DOS and OS/2 for IBM PCs and compatibles, and the Macintosh OS.

Optical character recognition: A process in which a device is used to scan a printed page to create a digital representation in the computer's memory. Special software is used to translate the digital images of letters and numbers into standard ASCII character codes, which then can be manipulated by word processors or other computer programs.

Optical storage: Storage technology which uses lasers to record and play back data at extremely high densities, for example on CD-ROM optical disks. It provides far greater storage capacity than magnetic storage media.

P

Parallel communications: A communications interface in which multiple bits of information are transferred on multiple parallel wires; typically used as the printer interface on IBM PC microcomputers for distances limited to 20 feet or less. See also Serial communications.

Parity: A simple error detection technique which uses a single binary bit to to verify the accuracy of data in computer memory and in data transfers.

Partition: An isolated segment of computer memory or disk drive capacity; partitions are used to separate unrelated or incompatible programs and data.

Patch: A method of repairing a faulty computer program which does not involve extensive rewriting or re-compilation of the program.

PC-DOS: See Operating system.

Peripheral equipment: External hardware devices, such as modems, printers, etc., that can be connected to a microcomputer system.

Piracy: The copying of software for use on microcomputers not covered by the software license.

Pixel: Picture element; refers to the individual dots that form an image on a display monitor.

Plotter: Peripheral device, similar to a printer, that uses a set of pens to draw a picture (generally graphs or charts) on paper or transparency film.

PostScript: A page description language created by Adobe Systems Inc.; used in printers to create high-quality typography and graphics.

Program: A set of instructions that direct the operations of a computer.

Project management: The process of tracking the resources and tasks associated with a given project.

Prompts: Messages displayed by a computer that instruct a user to input information or take action.

Protocol: Rules that relate to the methods for the orderly and reliable transmission of data over a communications network.

Public domain software: Software that is distributed by the author free of charge, usually through users groups and electronic bulletin boards.

Q

Queue: A list of actions or documents to be processed by a computer; "print queue" is often used to refer to a list of documents waiting to be printed.

QWERTY keyboard: The standard typewriter keyboard; refers to the first 6 letters of the top row of alphabetic characters.

R

Random access memory (RAM): The internal memory contained in a microcomputer, which can be written to or read from in any sequence.

Read-only memory (ROM): Internal memory in a computer containing information that is permanently stored and unalterable.

Rebooting: The process of restarting a computer after it has already been turned on, often to recover from a system crash. See also Cold boot, Crash, and Warm boot.

Recovery: The restoration of data and program files to a system after a crash or failure has been corrected.

RGB: A monitor using shades and combinations of the additive colors red, green, and blue to provide a full color display.

Remote access: The process of communicating with a computer from another computer or terminal that is located at a remote site.

Reset key: A button or key that erases all information from the internal RAM and restarts the computer.

RS-232-C: An ANSI technical specification for serial communication that establishes interface requirements between computers and modems or terminals; a standard type of computer cabling using 25-pin connectors.

S

Seek time: The amount of time required to position a disk drive's read mechanism to read the data on a specified disk track.

Serial communications: A communications interface in which data is transferred one bit at a time; although this method of transfer is slower than parallel communications, it is less expensive, has a broader range of applications, and can be used over longer distances.

Shareware: Software that is distributed by the author through users groups and bulletin board systems, and for which the author requests a small payment if the program is used regularly. Compare with Public domain software.

Software: A set of computer instructions (programs) that performs a specific task.

Spooling: The process of storing a set of data files or characters until the computer or peripheral can process them; printer spooling frees up the use of a computer while a long document is being printed.

Spreadsheet: A software application designed to store and manipulate numerical data; an electronic version of paper-based financial and accounting ledger systems.

SYLK: Symbolic link format; a format developed by Microsoft Corporation as a method of transferring data among spreadsheet applications.

Syntax error: An error in the instructions to a computer that results from incorrect use of programming language statements or system commands.

T

Tape drive: A mechanism that stores information on magnetic tape for later retrieval. Because tape is not a random access storage method, but has high levels of capacity, it is most often used for storage or archiving of data that will not be regularly accessed.

Telecommunications: The exchange of information between systems not located in the same facility.

Timesharing: The sharing of a single computer by several simultaneous users for different applications.

Topology: The physical interconnection arrangement of computers on a network, or the logical (functional) interconnections between the software programs that operate on the network. Examples are star, bus, and ring topologies.

Transaction processing: A type of processing that allows iterative processing of small programs and data, such to be interactively updated during data entry. See also Batch.

Transfer rate: The overall speed at which files or other information can be sent by a computer application program over a communications link.

Turnkey system: A computer system that is designed, configured, installed, and maintained by a single vendor for a specific application.

U

Universal Product Code (UPC): An identification system using unique bar codes that are read by an optical scanner.

UNIX: A very large and sophisticated multiuser operating system that runs on a variety of hardware platforms; developed by Bell Laboratories.

Unrecoverable error: An incorrect program instruction that results in abnormal termination of the program, such that the program and /or the computer itself must be reloaded and restarted.

Update: The modification of a file to reflect current information, or the distribution of revised or enhanced versions of computer software to users.

Upload: The process of sending a data file or program file over data communication lines to another computer. See also Download.

User group: An organization made up of individuals who share an interest in a particular computer system or application; members generally share information ranging from public domain software to newsletter articles.

Utility program: A program that performs a specialized but routine task such as sorting, updating, or backup.

V

Validation: For large and complex sets of manually entered data, the process by which errors and inconsistencies are detected and/or eliminated by running the data through a specialized software program,

VAR: Value-Added Reseller; a vendor that repackages or enhances hardware from an Original Equipment Manufacturer and resells it to users at a higher price.

VDT: A video display terminal; used as a generic term for any computer display monitor.

Videotex: A computer-based system for distribution of information and/or services in the form of alphanumeric text and/or graphics to consumers equipped with personal computers or low cost display terminals.

Virtual memory: A technique for using magnetic storage media in such a way that it appears to the program as random access memory. Virtual memory allows programs to manipulate large amounts of data which would otherwise not fit in the available memory.

Volatile memory: Memory chips that lose the information stored in them when power is removed. See also Dynamic RAM.

W

Wait state: A pause in the operation of a central processing unit, usually the length of one instruction cycle of the processor; wait states occur when the processor must wait for slower speed components of the computer (often memory chips) to complete their operations.

Warm boot: The process of restarting a computer without turning off the electrical power or without re-loading the computer's operating software into memory. See also Cold boot.

Winchester disk: See Hard disk.

Window: A display area on a screen that provides a view of a specific document or operation; used in operating systems or programs that provide multiple views of a document or multitasking of programs.

Word processor: A computer system or software application that provides text editing and output facilities.

Word wrap: In a text based application program, a feature which causes text to "wrap" around to the next line when the end of a line is reached.

X

Xenix: A form of the multiuser operating system UNIX, developed by Microsoft Corporation specifically for use in an IBM PC microcomputer environment. See also UNIX.

Xmodem: A popular data communications protocol for file transfer and error-checking.

Appendix B

Bibliography

Management

Anglin, Richard V. "Computer commandments: cooperate and plan before you buy anything." *Library Journal*, v. 109, Oct. 1, 1984, p. 1821 (2).

Ansfield, Paul J. "Humanizing the installation of microcomputers." *Catholic Library World*, v. 54, Nov. 1982, p. 151 (4).

Becker, Karen A. "CD-ROM: a primer." *College & Research Libraries News*, v. 48, July/Aug. 1987, p. 388 (5).

Bothwell, Isobel, and Frances Lovejoy. "Technological change: experiences and opinions of library workers." *Australian Academic and Research Libraries*, v. 18, Mar. 1987, p. 41 (7).

Buis, Vern. "Selecting printers and modems." *OCLC Micro*, v. 5, Feb. 1, 1989, p. 19 (3).

Burton, Paul F. *The librarian's guide to microcomputer for information management*. Workingham, England and New York, Van Nostrand Reinhold, 1986. 271 p.

Cargill, Jennifer. "Paying attention to basics: selecting microcomputer hardware and software." *Technicalities*, v. 7, Oct. 1987, p. 8 (3).

Cole, David H. "Putting micros to work: one library's checklist." *Small Computers in Libraries,* v. 7, Feb. 1987, p. 24 (3).

Connecting with technology 1988: microcomputers in libraries. (Supplement to *Small Computers in Libraries,* No. 8) Westport, CT, 1988.

Costa, Betty, and Marie Costa. *A micro handbook for small libraries and media centers.* Littleton, CO, Libraries Unlimited, 1983. 216 p.

Craghill, Denise. "Information technology and staff deployment in public libraries." *CRUS News,* v. 31, July 1988, p. 8 (3).

Davis, David M. "Public access microcomputer services in public libraries." *Library Journal,* v. 112, Nov. 1, 1987, p. 56 (8).

Dewey, Patrick R. *101 software packages to use in your library.* Chicago, American Library Association, 1987. 160 p.

———. *Microcomputers and the reference librarian.* Westport, CT, Meckler, 1989. 207 p.

Dyer, Hilary. *A directory of library and information retrieval software for microcomputers.* Brookfield, VT, Gower, 1988. 75 p.

Dykhuis, Randy. *Template directory for libraries, 1989-1990.* Westport, CT, Meckler, 1989.

Falk, Howard. *Personal computers for libraries.* Medford, NJ, Learned Information, 1985. 174 p.

Foster, Susan. "Technological shock is manageable." *Personal Computing,* v. 6, Feb. 1982, p. 55 (4).

Golfer, J. Larry. "Going online with America: the world of electronic bulletin boards, part I." *Small Computers in Libraries,* v. 6, Feb. 1986, p. 20 (4).

Hall, Hal W. "Microcomputer centers in libraries: staffing considerations." *Library Software Review,* v. 5, Nov./Dec. 1986, p. 341 (3).

Harrell, Jeanne. "Revolutionizing acquisitions productivity with PC's." *Technicalities,* v. 7, Oct. 1987, p. 3 (5).

Holloway, Carson, and Margaret Jackson. "Microcomputer data files for libraries: a selected bibliography." *Online*, v. 13, Jan. 1989, p. 59 (6).

Jackson, Lillian. "Automating the circulation at Dana Library: effects on the staff and the public." *Journal of Education for Library and Information Science*, v. 28, Spring 1988, p. 276 (4).

Kilpatrick, Thomas L. *Microcomputers and libraries*. Metuchen, NJ, Scarecrow Press, 1987. 726 p.

Kington, Robert A. "Responding to an RFP: a vendor's viewpoint." *Library Hi Tech*, v. 5, Spring 1987, p. 61 (5).

Kirby, Christine L. "Preparing grant proposals for automation funding." *Bulletin of the American Society for Information Science*, v. 12, Aug./Sept. 1988, p. 17 (2).

Kline, Norman. "Acquisition decision analysis, or how to make a good purchase." *Small Computers in Libraries*, v. 7, Jan. 1987, p. 16 (3).

Learn, Larry L. "The OCLC network: its architecture, application, and operation." *Library Hi Tech*, v. 6, Sept. 1, 1988, p. 43 (18).

"Library workstations." *Wilson Library Bulletin*, v. 63, Oct. 1988, p. 22 (35).

Mason, Robert M. "The micro manager." *Library Journal*, v. 109, Apr. 15, 1984, p 794 (2).

Matthews, Joseph R, Stephen R. Salmon, and Joan Frye Williams. "The RFP—request for punishment: or a tool for selecting an automated library system." *Library Hi Tech*, v. 5, Spring 1987, p. 15 (7).

McClean, Neil. "A bigger slice: cost justification for library and information services." *Aslib Proceedings*, v. 39, Oct. 1987, p. 293 (5).

Microcomputers for library decision making: issues, trends, and applications. Edited by Peter Hernon and Charles R. McClure. Norwood, NJ, Ablex, 1986. 311 p.

Moran, T. P. "An applied psychology of the user." *ACM Computing Surveys*, v. 13, Mar. 1981, p. 1 (11).

Nelson, Nancy Melin. " 'Our' profession in the pre-information age." *Information Today*, v. 6, June 1, 1989, p. 29 (3).

Oakley, Robert. "Microcomputers for more than on-line searching: some cautionary notes." *Law Library Journal*, v. 79, Spring 1987, 335 (9).

Palmer, Roger C. *Understanding library microcomputer systems*. Studio City, CA, Pacific Information, 1988. 128 p.

Public access microcomputers in academic libraries. Chicago, American Library Association, 1987. 209 p.

Public technology: the library public access computer. (Essential guide to Apple computers in libraries, Vol. 1) Edited by Jean Armour Polly. Westport, CT, Meckler, 1986. 169 p.

Raitt, David I. "P's and C's of PCs." *Microcomputers for Information Management.*, v. 4, Mar. 1987, p. 1 (10).

Robertson, Steven D. *Public microcomputing*. Studio City, CA, Pacific Information, 1986. 102 p.

Rooks, Dana C. "Implementing the automated acquisitions system: perspectives of a personnel administrator." *Library Acquisitions: Practice and Theory*, v. 12, no. 3/4, 1988, p. 431 (7).

Rush, James E. "The library automation market: why do vendors fail?" *Library Hi Tech*, v. 6, Sept. 1, 1988, p. 61 (6).

Saffady, William. "The Macintosh as a library workstation: a report on available hardware and software." *Library Technology Reports*, v. 23, Jan.-Feb. 1987, p. 5 (191).

Schroeder, Penny. "Implementing the automated acquisitions system: staffing considerations." *Library Acquisitions: Practice and Theory*, v. 12, no. 3/4, 1988, p. 423 (6).

Siitonen, Leena. "Assimilating the microcomputer: the use of microcomputers in public library services." *Journal of Educational Media & Library Sciences.*, v. 25, Winter 1988, p. 111 (21).

Stewart, Linda, Katherine S. Chiang, and Bill Coons. *Public access CD-ROMs in libraries: case studies*. Westport, CT, Meckler, 1990. 328 p.

Technology for the nineties. (Supplement to *Computers in Libraries*, No. 15). Edited by Nancy Melin Nelson. Westport, CT, Meckler, 1989.

Uppgard, Jeannine. *Developing microcomputer work areas in academic libraries.* (Supplement to *Small Computers in Libraries*, No. 5) Westport, CT, Meckler, 1988.

Maintenance

Beechhold, Henry F. *The Brady guide to microcomputer troubleshooting and maintenance.* New York, Prentice Hall, 1987. 324 p.

———. *The plain English repair and maintenance guide for home computers.* New York, Simon & Schuster, 1984. 265 p.

———. *The plain English repair and maintenance guide for IBM personal computers.* New York, Simon & Schuster, 1985. 259 p.

Beiser, Karl. "Micro housekeeping." *Small Computers in Libraries,* v. 6, Jan. 1986, p. 7 (5).

Brenner, Robert C. *The Apple II Plus/IIe troubleshooting & repair guide.* Indianapolis, H.W. Sams, 1984. 259 p.

———. *IBM PC advanced troubleshooting & repair.* Indianapolis, H.W. Sams, 1988. 289 p.

Brill, Kenneth. "Site uptime management: an ounce of disaster prevention is worth a pound of cure." *Computerworld,* v. 21, June 3, 1987, p. 33 (3).

Close, Mary. "Micro maintenance: keeping your computer healthy." *Small Computers in Libraries,* v. 7, Feb. 1987, p. 27 (3).

Danuloff, Craig, and Deke McClelland. *Encyclopedia Macintosh.* Alameda, CA, Sybex, 1990. 782 p.

Esparza, Mary S. "Computer maintenance: bypassing politics." *Infosystems,* v. 34, Sept. 1987, p. 51 (3).

Fowler, Eric S. "The aging PC, the '286, the '386, OS/2 and you." *Small Computers in Libraries,* v. 8, May 1988, p. 20 (7).

Glass, Brett L. "Hard disk maintenance software." *BYTE,* v. 14, Aug. 1, 1989, p. 265 (8).

Heid, Jim. "Getting started with basic maintenance." *Macworld,* v. 4, July 1987, p. 185 (5).

Hoffman, Jake. "Maintenance contracts: should you or shouldn't you?" *Small Computers in Libraries*, v. 7, Sept. 1987, p. 15 (4).

Jackway, Ken. *How to keep the darn things running.* Scottsdale, AZ, Computer Fix-It Workshops, 1986. 202 p.

Kane, Pamela. *V.I.R.U.S. protection: vital information resources under siege.* New York, Bantam, 1989. 477 p.

Kay, Emily. "Lack of formal backup strategies plagues many installations." *PC Week*, v. 5, July 4, 1988, p. 79 (3).

Kersey, Roger. *Personal computer operation and troubleshooting.* Englewood Cliffs, NJ, Prentice Hall, 1989. 354 p.

Ludlum, David A. "Navigating the PC service maze." *Computerworld*, v. 23, Feb. 20, 1989, p. 103 (1).

Margolis, Art. *Troubleshooting and repairing the new personal computers.* Blue Ridge Summit, PA, 1987. 401 p.

Mertan, Alan D. "Technician's tips on maintenance." *Classroom Computer Learning*, v. 6 , Sept. 1985, p. 40 (2).

Mueller, Scott. *Upgrading and repairing PCs.* Carmel, IN, Oue Corp., 1988. 724 p.

Purcell, Royal. "Micros in vocational-technical centers: some tips from an expert." *Small Computers in Libraries*, v. 8, Mar. 1988, p. 23 (2).

Sandberg-Diment, Erik. "All right, let's keep it clean." *New York Times*, v. 136, Feb. 1, 1987, p. 20F(1).

Stephenson, John G. *Microcomputer troubleshooting & repair.* Indianapolis, H.W. Sams, 1988. 354 p.

Williams, Gene B. *Chilton's guide to Macintosh repair and maintenance.* Radnor, PA, Chilton Book Co., 1986. 212 p.

———. *Chilton's guide to small computer repair and maintenance.* Radnor, PA, Chilton Book Co., 1986. 171 p.

———. *How to repair and maintain your Apple computer.* Radnor, PA, Chilton Book Co., 1985. 212 p.

Appendix C

Current Journals

Library-oriented journals

CD-ROM Librarian
Meckler Corporation
11 Ferry Lane West
Westport, CT 06880

   Focuses on the use of CD-ROM technology in libraries. Includes industry news, product reviews, reports on conferences, and bibliographies. Published 11 times per year.

Computers in Libraries
Meckler Corporation
11 Ferry Lane West
Westport, CT 06880

   A newsletter containing articles on practical procedures and applications for using microcomputers in libraries. Also features reviews of applicable books, periodicals and software. Published 11 times per year.

Electronic Library
Learned Information, Inc.
143 Old Marlton Pike
Medford, NJ 08055

For librarians and information center managers interested in microcomputers and library automation. Articles on a broad range of pertinent topics. Features include industry news and product announcements. Published bimonthly.

Information Technology and Libraries
c/o Library and Information Technology Association
50 East Huron St.
Chicago, IL 60611

Publishes material related to all aspects of library and information technology. Some specific topics of interest include computerized information technology, data management, library networks, storage and retrieval systems, and systems analysis. Published quarterly.

Library Hi Tech
Library Hi Tech News
Pierian Press
P.O. Box 1808
Ann Arbor, MI 48106

This pair of publications address applications of technology in the library environment. *Library Hi Tech* includes feature articles highlighting specific library projects and views of industry trends. It is published quarterly. *Library Hi Tech News* focuses on industry news, including information on new products and policies.

Library Software Review
Meckler Corporation
11 Ferry Lane West
Westport, CT 06880

For libraries and educators. Articles cover the topics of software evaluation, procurement, applications and installation decisions. Published bi-monthly.

Library Workstation Report
Meckler Corporation
11 Ferry Lane West
Westport, CT 06880

Covers library management and collection access applications. Provides information on developments, trends and use of DOS-based and Macintosh workstations in the library as well as available and developing software packages. Published monthly (combined issues July/August and November/December).

Microcomputers for Information Management
Ablex Publishing Corp.
355 Chestnut Street
Norwood, NJ 07648

For librarians and information specialists. Features articles on the applications of microcomputers in information processing, organization, and dissemination as well as information on microcomputer hardware and software. Published quarterly.

Technicalities
M.E. Sharpe, Inc.
80 Business Park Drive
Armonk, NY 10504

A newsletter focusing on the use of technology in libraries. Includes articles on the impact of technology in the library and information science environment, as well as review articles. Published monthly.

Popular journals

Byte
Subscriber Service
P.O. Box 551
Hightstown, NJ 08520
Focuses on the technical aspects of microcomputers, but is not limited to specific brands or configurations of equipment. Often contains detailed specifications of the internal components of equipment, and addresses the needs of computer experts. Published 13 times a year.

MacUser
P.O. Box 56986
Boulder, CO 80321-6986
800-627-2247
Provides information on the Macintosh line of microcomputers. Includes sections designed for beginners, as well as for "power users." Quarterly summary of product reviews in tear-out form. Published 12 times a year.

MacWorld
c/o IDG Communications, Inc.
501 Second Street
San Francisco, CA 94107
Covers a wide range of general issues relating to use of the Macintosh line of computers. Includes product reviews and how-to sections. Published 12 times a year.

PC Magazine
P.O. Box 54093
Boulder, CO 80322
800-289-0429

Covers a broad range of issues related to the use of IBM-PC and compatible computers. It includes comprehensive product reviews, how-to features, and a number of regular columns on the industry. Published 22 times a year.

PC World
PCW Communications, Inc.
501 Second Street, Suite 600
San Francisco, CA 94107

Examines products and trends in the microcomputer industry as they relate to use of the IBM-PC and compatible computers. Includes product reviews and how-tos. Published 12 times a year.

PC/Computing
P.O Box 58229
Boulder, CO 80321-8229
800-365-2770

Emphasizes the social and organizational aspects of microcomputer use, focusing primarily on the use of IBM-PC and compatible microcomputers. Includes product reviews, analyses of trends in computing, and how-to sections. Published 12 times a year.

Appendix D

Organizations & Online Services

Library technology organizations

ASIS
American Society for Information Science
1424 16th Street, N.W.
Suite 404
Washington, DC 20036

ASIS draws its membership not only from the library community, but also from other information science areas such as computer science and engineering. The focus of its activities are upon the impact of information science and technology upon all facets of organizational development.

Library and Information Technology Association (LITA)
Library Administration and Management Association (LAMA)
c/o American Library Association
50 East Huron St.
Chicago, IL 60611

These two divisions of ALA focus most closely on the issues of microcomputer management and use in libraries. Their committees, interest groups, programs, and publications provide librarians with important contacts and information that can assist in the process of managing a microcomputer facility.

Online services and bulletin board systems

ALIX (Automated Library Information eXchange)
c/o Fedlink
Library of Congress
Washington, DC 20840
1-202-707-9656

One of the few library-oriented bulletin board services. ALIX was created for Federal librarians, but is open to the general public. Excellent discussion of library-related computer issues, and a useful library of applications and data files.

CompuServe
5000 Arlington Centre Blvd.
Columbus, OH 43220
1-800-848-8990 (in Ohio, or outside the U.S., call 1-614-457-8650)

CompuServe is a for-profit online service which provides access to a wide range of discussion forums and databases.

LITA Microcomputer Users Group Conference
c/o Elizabeth Lane
Congressional Information Service, EDP Dept.
4520 East-West Hwy, Suite 800
Bethesda, MD 20814

An online discussion conference devoted to the issue of microcomputer use in libraries. Started for members of the Microcomputer Users Interest Group of LITA, it has been expanded to include all those interested in the use of microcomputer technology in libraries.

Index

Software
>and local area networks 14, 28
>cataloging 27
>circulation 27, 104
>costs 66
>evaluation 27, 48
>evaluations 10
>file recovery applications 147
>installation of 83
>licensing agreements 66, 105
>licensing of 100
>policies for use 99
>public domain 3, 67, 122
>requirements 37
>security of 33, 81
>shareware 3, 67
>users groups 2
>vaporware 49

Software applications 48
>backup programs 128
>database management 23
>disk utilities 124
>electronic mail 23
>graphics 57
>library functions 25
>screen savers 122
>spreadsheets 23
>telecommunications 23, 56
>virus prevention, detection and eradication 130, 148
>word processing 22

Staffing needs 33, 69, 98
>public access facilities 27, 99